D1626131

CHILDHOOD IN INDIA

CHILDHOOD IN INDIA
Tales from Sholapur

George Roche

Presented and Edited by
Richard Terrell

The Radcliffe Press
London · New York

Published in 1994 by
The Radcliffe Press
45 Bloomsbury Square
London WC1A 2HY

175 Fifth Avenue
New York
NY 10010

In the United States of America
and Canada distributed by
St Martin's Press
175 Fifth Avenue
New York
NY 10010

A full CIP record for this book is available from the British Library

Library of Congress Catalog card number: 94–60178
A full CIP record is available from the Library of Congress

ISBN 1–85043–791–2

Copy-edited and laser-set by Selro Publishing Services, Oxford
Printed and bound in Great Britain by WBC Ltd, Bridgend, Mid Glamorgan

TO THE SOVEREIGNTY OF REASON IN AN AGE
OF CONFLICTING IDENTITIES

G.R.
R.T.

Contents

Illustrations

General Foreword
to the Series

Anthony Kirk-Greene MBE

Emeritus Fellow of St Antony's College, Oxford University, and
formerly of the Colonial Administrative Service, Nigeria

A whole generation has passed, nearer two in the case of the Asian sub-continent, since Britain's colonial territories in South-East Asia, Africa and the Caribbean achieved independence. In the Pacific the transfer of power came about a decade later. There was little interest in recording the official or the personal experience of empire either in the inter-war years — viewed by some, often among those personally involved, as the apogee of the British empire — or in the immediate aftermath of empire. And in this latter period attitudes were largely critical, largely condemnatory and even positively hostile. This is not surprising: such a reaction is usual at the end of a remarkable period of history.

With the passing of time and with longer historical perspective it was possible to see events in a better and more objective light and the trend was gradually reversed. In due course there came about a more sympathetic interest in the colonial period, both in Britain and in the countries of the former empire, among those who were intrigued to know how colonial government operated — in local, everyday practice, as well as at the policy level of the Colonial Office and Government House. Furthermore, those who had themselves been an integral part of the process wanted to record the experience before, in the nature of things, it was too late. Here was a potentially rich vein of knowledge and personal experience for specialist academic historians as well as the general reader.

Leaving aside the extensive academic analysis of the end of empire, the revival of interest in the colonial period in this country may be said to have been stimulated by creative literature. In the late 1960s there were novels, films and radio and TV programmes, now and again tinged with a touch of nineteenth-century romance and with just a whiff of nostalgia to soften the sharp realism of the colonial encounter. The focus was primarily on India and the post-1947 imagery of the 'Raj': there were outstanding novels by Paul Scott — surely destined to be one of the greatest twentieth-century novelists — J. G. Farrell and John Masters; epic films like *A Passage to India* and *Gandhi*, the charming and moving vignette of *Staying On*, and, for Africa, *Out of Africa* and *Mister Johnson*.

In the second half of the 1970s there emerged a highly successful genre of collective 'colonial' memoirs in the *Tales of ...* format: Charles Allen's splendid trilogy *Plain Tales from the Raj* (1975), *Tales from the Dark Continent* (1979) and *Tales from the South China Seas* (1983), followed by others like *Tales of Paradise: Memories of the British in the South Pacific* (1986) and *Tales of Empire: The British in the Middle East* (1989), all good history and good reading.

Throughout the period from India's independence until that of the last crown colony there had, of course, been those splendid works which combined both academic history and creative literature: for example, Philip Woodruff's *Men who Ruled India: The Founders* (1953) and *The Guardians* (1954); and Jan Morris's *Heaven's Command, Pax Britannica* and *Farewell the Trumpets* (1973–8).

Finally, as the 1970s gave way to the 1980s, those voices which had remained largely silent since the end of empire now wanted to be heard. The one-time colonial officials, be they district officers, agriculturalists, veterinary, medical or forestry officers, policemen or magistrates, and just as often their wives, began to write about their experiences. They wrote with relish and enthusiasm, with a touch of adventure and few personal regrets. There was a common feeling of a practical and useful task well done, although some thought that more could have been achieved had independence come about more slowly.

These memoirs often began as little more than a private record for the family, children and grandchildren, some of who had never seen a colonial governor in full fig, shaken hands with an emir or paramount chief, discussed plans with a peasant or local politician, or known at first hand the difference between an *askari* and an *alkali*, an *amah* and an *ayah*. By 1990, the colonial memoir had begun to establish itself as a literary genre in its own right.

The initiative of the Radcliffe Press in harnessing and promoting this talent, primarily autobiographical but also biographical, promises to be a positive addition to both the historical and the literary scenes. Here are voices from the last Colonial Service generation, relating from personal experience the lives and careers involved in the exercise of latter-day empire. They were part of what was arguably the most influential and far-reaching international event of the second half of the twentieth century, namely the end of empire and the consequent emergence of the independent nations of the Third World. It could also perhaps be argued that this is part of an even greater process — decolonization 'writ large', a sea-change in world affairs affecting greater and lesser powers into the late twentieth century.

It may well be that by 2066, the centenary of the closing down of the Colonial Office, great-great-grandchildren will find the most telling image of Britain's third and final empire in these authentic memoirs and biographical studies, rather than in the weightier imperial archives at the Public Record Office at Kew or in Rhodes House Library, Oxford.

Acknowledgements

I paid many visits to the India Office Library and Records to discover details associated with George's memoir, including such matters as the history of the princely state of Akalkot since the middle of the last century, the precise location of many of the places mentioned in the text, such as Sholapur, Washimbi, Mahabeleshwar, Khonoor and the Nilgiri Hills. I am grateful to Mr T. Thomas, Mr I. A. Baxter, Dr R. Bingle and Mr Martin Moir, formerly Deputy Director of the Library and Records and now retired.

For information about the princely family of Akalkot and the use now made of the former palace buildings after the abolition of all the princely states by the newly independent government of India in 1949–50, I applied to the India High Commission and to the Government of India Tourist Office in London, but neither authority was able to supply any information whatever, despite correspondence with India on my behalf.

In some frustration I mentioned my inquiries to a personal friend, Alfred Silvertown, whose wife is of Indian birth. Mrs Silvertown has a niece, Mrs Fleur Madnani, who lives in Bombay where she represents an international trading company. I was advised to write to her. I did so with special interest after learning that Fleur Madnani, a few years ago, had been elected as Miss India in one of the famous Miss World beauty competitions.

Mrs Madnani, who has business contacts in Akalkot, succeeded in corresponding with Mr G. Bagul, Secretary to the Royal Family of Akalkot, who lives in the new palace. I am most grateful to Alfred Silvertown and his wife, to Mrs Fleur Madnani and to Mr Bagul for the information recorded in the eqilogue below.

As a fellow member of The British Association for Cemeteries in South Asia, I asked Mr Peter de Jong if he could advise me on how to set about the problem of searching for the grave and possible tombstone of Roberta Roche, the very beautiful mother of the three children described in these pages. Mr de Jong has nobly undertaken to deal with all inquiries about cemeteries and tombs in Southern India, including Maharashtra and the Deccan. He advised me to write to the Revd M. A. Daniel of the Methodist Church in Poona who is the honorary secretary of the Poona Cemeteries Committee, and I did so. In his reply the Revd Daniel informed me that he had traced the grave to a particular cemetery. The tombstone of marble was in good condition and the inscription recording the full names of Roberta Roche, her dates of birth and death, being quite legible.

This was gratifying, but I wanted more precise information. I asked the Revd Daniel if he could describe the tombstone and perhaps send me a photograph of it, and let me have the exact wording of the inscription. Peter de Jong also requested the Revd Daniel to send a photograph. I received no response to my letter for nearly two months.

During this hiatus I met Martin Moir (see the first photograph above) in the street in London. He had just returned from a visit to India. He said he would write to a Jesuit friend in Bombay who might know how to trace the tomb of Roberta Roche.

Shortly afterwards I received a letter from a man in Poona who may be a relative of the Revd M. A. Daniel, namely Father Lourdes Daniel of the Church of Our Lady of Perpetual Help. He informed me that the grave is in the Faith Sulpice cemetery on the Sholapur Road, and quoted the inscription in full.

Within a day or two I received another letter from the Revd M. A. Daniel, enclosing two excellent photographs of the grave and the full inscription. He had just returned from a long holiday with his family, and had not seen my letter until his return to Poona.

My warm thanks go to the Revd M. A. Daniel, to Father Lourdes Daniel, to the Jesuit friend of Martin Moir in Bombay, to Martin Moir himself and, of course to Peter de Jong in London.

For all the stories and incidents recorded in this book I shall always be grateful to George and Kathleen Roche, whose friendship I retain though we have not been able to meet for the last 40 years.

R.T.
London

Author's Preface

I was born in India in 1915, and for the first 12 years of my life I thought of it as home. My parents had taken me and my brother and sister on leave with them to England, the grey place they called home. However, England had not actually been home to very many of their ancestors, who had roots all over Europe. My father's grandfather came from France to England in about the year 1837, and his grandmother's parents had come from Prague to England in about 1825.

I was sent to a boarding school in England in 1927, an experience I prefer to forget. I went on to London University and in 1939 I joined the Royal Engineers. I was almost immediately posted to India, but not for long. I saw active service in the desert and in Italy. After the war I was posted to India again, and to Palestine for a while. When I left the army in 1948, I joined HM Overseas Civil Service and served in Nigeria, Malaya and (after a short break with a private company in Pakistan) in Zambia.

I have much to look back upon, with many memories of many places. But of all my memories I hold those of my childhood in India the most dear. This book is for my grandchildren, who never had such an experience, and for my brother and sister who shared it all with me.

(G.R.)

Editor's Introduction

I first met George Roche and his wife Kathleen in Nigeria in 1952, during a spell of two years when I had been temporarily transferred to the Colonial Administrative Service in that country from my permanent job in the Colonial Office in Whitehall.

Although I had not met him before, I was already aware of his existence. For back in the office my job had been to deal with the applications of candidates for appointments in the service who appeared (mostly on paper, but sometimes on the basis of interviews as well) to be suitable for particular vacancies. In the post-war years the British government (socialist at first) required the administrations of all the overseas dependencies, numbering over 40 widely scattered countries, to concoct ten-year development programmes, the idea largely inspired by the five-year plans of the Soviet Union. Post-war euphoria about building a better world was extremely infectious, and few of us in Whitehall, or in the territories themselves, escaped it. Anyway, I had been struck by the unusual combination of qualifications Roche seemed to possess for any one of a large number of vacancies in the service, especially in the Northern region of Nigeria.

There were two special things to remember about this man of my imagination. First, a moral quality. He had been mentioned in despatches for certain acts of daring, bravery and efficiency during the campaign against Rommel's forces in North Africa in 1942, when he had been a captain in the

Royal Engineers. He soon became a major and remained in the army till some time after the war. I had sent for the despatch describing his achievements, but recall from recent correspondence rather more than is contained in the citation.

During the long withdrawal towards Egypt before the advancing Germans, George was captured at Mersa Matruh, where he had been in charge of the destruction of British ammunition dumps, to prevent them falling into the hands of the enemy. He was sent to Tobruk to be shipped to a prisoner of war camp in Italy, but managed to escape. He was recaptured but again escaped and, with four comrades, managed somehow to cross 400 kilometres of desert to rejoin the British forces at El Alamein, in which battle he was able to take part.

Stationed in England after the war George was engaged in important staff work involving the postings of engineers all over the world. Eventually he tired of peacetime army life and filled in one of my complicated forms of application to join the administrative service overseas.

Second, before the war he had passed the BSc (Civil Engineering) intermediate examination at the University of London, before switching over to natural science (botany and chemistry) for his final degree.

When assessing the suitability of an applicant for any kind of job, we do not usually apply strictly logical procedures. Logically, there is no convincing reason why a man who had been brave, and even efficient, in war should become a humane and wise administrator in peacetime, or vice versa. And, indeed, many brave and decorated officers turned out to be impetuous and awkward figures in their subsequent affairs, domestic or vocational, or both. However, I was looking for qualities of leadership, more important than any other human quality in the administration of great stretches of rural Africa. No development schemes, economic, social, educational or constitutional can be effective in any part of the world unless those responsible for introducing and managing them can inspire the confidence of the people of the country they are designed to serve. I sensed that George could do so.

George's academic qualifications were unusual. The higher education of most candidates, with or without degrees, was in such subjects as history, literature, classics, economics, languages and perhaps law. All these subjects were conducive to achievement in an important phase of administration, namely the ability to explain complex matters in simple, accurate writing for the benefit of others, usually superiors. This leads to a certain kind of ambition, very understandable when an officer is married with a couple of small children. He wants to live in a centre equipped with houses, furnishings and reasonably clear looking water.

I knew, however, that we needed especially the kinds of men who could persuade the inhabitants of an African village to build a dry-season road for 20 miles across a stretch of waterless bush, to enable a lorry to collect their newly grown cotton crop and take it to a new ginnery. Or perhaps to dig a deep well in stifling heat when there was no money to pay anybody any wages. Such achievements were called 'community development', and were often very successful, to the intellectual confusion of certain experts in London or New York. The officer who could draft a well-composed letter beneath an electric fan might never succeed in cracking a joke in Hausa or Fulani with a dozen villagers, none of whom could read or write.

In Africa, George's practical knowledge of engineering, gathered in war conditions, enabled him to take on a large district almost single-handed. He knew how to make a useful bridge across a muddy stream, how to make a road with proper embankments, gutters, cuttings and culverts, or what to do about a flood, or a couple of broken-down lorries. And his understanding of botany and general ecology enabled him to teach peasants how to cultivate their frail, sandy soil without letting it get washed away in the heavy storms of the rainy season.

Stationed by pure chance in the same province as George, I found him an excellent friend, able to help me in many practical ways. When anything went wrong with my car in a large country almost devoid of public transport, he would know what was probably wrong and tell me how to put it right. When I received some packets of seeds for flowers and vegetables from England, and wanted to make a garden round my little asbestos and cement bungalow on completely virgin bush land, he knew just where they should be planted, at what depth, and how to make the best use of a locally available manure. Unlike a great many British officers at that time, who were often cold and distant in their dealings with Africans, George was obviously very popular with them. Other officers would curry favour with their superiors in the service; George was always able to get the support of Africans in any project concerning them. He had a wonderful flair for picking up local African dialects, and an ever-ready sense of humour, which they enjoyed.

In 1953, George resigned from the colonial service to take up an appointment with the Bombay Burmah Corporation, and went to Pakistan to recruit former members of his old regiment, the Royal Engineers, to work in the forests of North Borneo. Eventually he returned to the colonial service in Africa in various central African territories. He retired some years ago after a manifestly adventurous career.

Readers will want to know how George came to write his memoir of his childhood in India and what part I have played in the making of this book. Since my own retirement early in 1969, I have written a few autobiographical books about personal experience in India and in West Africa. George and his wife read them, which prompted him to write a memoir of his own. His motive, however, was not of a literary nature. As he says in his preface, his main concern was to enable his own descendants to share his memories with him, memories of a kind never to be repeated

Kathleen Roche typed out his memoirs to George's dictation and posted them to me in bundles. He described the episodes with little concern for their chronological sequence, which was sometimes awkward to work out. George's style was not literary, but essentially oral and often colloquial. Nevertheless, the memoirs were so fascinating that I felt determined somehow to get them published as a contribution to the annals of the British Raj, belonging to the same epoch as those of E. M. Forster (whose *A Passage to India* was first published in 1924).

It is important that the reader of this book should at least be reminded of the broad sequence of events that had already begun to unfold in the years of George's memoir. The events were numerous and complex, but can be regarded as of two main kinds. Ever since the last decades of the nineteenth century, most political and intellectual leaders, Indian and British alike, had become aware of a future in which the Indian Empire of Britain would be succeeded by something else. It was not until 1946, after the Second World War, that the prospect of full constitutional independence of the whole sub-continent was almost universally accepted.

The two kinds of events to which I refer were these. First, even before the end of the First World War, the Liberal government of Britain decided that, however the constitutional status of India might be defined, an ever-increasing number of qualified Indians should participate in the daily work of government at all levels and in all fields. This policy was described as the 'Montagu-Chelmsford Reforms' (Edwin Montagu being the Secretary of State for India in London and Lord Chelmsford being the Viceroy in Calcutta). It was steadily implemented over the decades and was perhaps the most important of the policies leading eventually to the independence of India after the Second World War. It was subject to review every ten years, and the pace of 'Indianization' actually applied varied between the different branches of government. It was relatively slow in the services responsible for the maintenance of order (for example, the armed forces and the police), and quicker in such branches as taxation, education, rural administration, law and justice.

The other kind of events were in the constitutional field. Here the main problems were those of finding a method of holding the country together whilst British authority was progressively withdrawn, and, of course, coping with the speed of the process as a whole. There was no single dominant language, and among the Indians themselves people had conflicting feelings of national unity, not to mention their conflicting religions, communities, castes and military traditions. There was little agreement, among either Indian or British leaders, about what measures were needed to prevent the break-up of the sub-continent into warring fragments as the British withdrew.[1] The present ghastliness of the fate of the former Yugoslavia haunted our forebears, Indian and British alike, on a vast scale. Starting in 1931 a series of 'Round Table Conferences' were held in London, to which representatives of all the various group interests were invited, in the hope of arriving at agreed constitutional objectives. This led to the India Act of 1935, which provided for a form of self-government, or autonomy, at the provincial level, after local elections of great importance were held in 1937. The outbreak of the Second World War interrupted the process, mainly because of the need for defence both against the

1. During a long visit to India in 1980 I was suddenly asked by an Indian friend why Britain had so suddenly abandoned her empire in the few years after the Second World War, instead of defending it to the last ditch, as imperialists are supposed to do. My impromptu reply to that challenging question, which much concerns the Indian bloodbath of 1946/7, may interest some readers. See pp.116–17 of my book, *A Perception of India* (1984).

Japanese in the East and against the Germans and Italians in the West. In those years India was a great military base. When independence came in 1947 its arrival was celebrated in a bloodbath the responsibility for which is disputed, but that lies beyond the horizons of this book.

I have learnt during recent months more about George Roche than I ever knew in Nigeria. I then knew nothing about his Indian childhood, his parents and their forebears on both sides. At an early stage I asked him to tell me something about his ancestry. In response he sent me two enormous genealogical tables going back more than two centuries, the tables having been made with great care by one of his cousins a few years ago. They contain hundreds of names of individuals who lived right across the European continent including the British Isles. As will be seen, George's maternal grandfather was born in Madras of Armenian Christian lineage of great antiquity. Since all this material was too abundant to be included in this kind of book, I asked George to see if he could make a brief prose summary, which he did. I have added a note to it mentioning various forebears whom he omitted from his summary, perhaps because he did not wish to be charged with name-dropping.

This book is a joint product of George and myself. In preparing the text, with its many footnotes, I have come to live with George's memories as though they were my own. Perhaps other readers will share this moving experience. Nostalgic it certainly is, but so is every interest in the subject known as history.

1

Hardwar

I t was early in October 1918, towards the end of the monsoon. A new freshness could be felt in the atmosphere after the steamy heat of previous weeks, and the Indian countryside was now lush and green. The Ganges canal, an irrigation artery for vast tracts of the United Provinces, was flowing swift and deep.

These were the days of the 'Mela' festivals in Hardwar, when vast numbers of Hindus streamed into the town from the surrounding villages to rejoice at the fertility promised for the growing season, and to purify themselves in the water of holy Mother Ganges, flowing in the canal. Among the pilgrims was a bridging unit commanded by my father, Captain Robert Roche, an officer of the Royal Engineers serving with the Bengal Sappers and Miners. They formed part of the Indian Army, but still retained the name of 'Bengal', derived from the past before the Indian Mutiny of 1857/8, when the East India Company possessed three separate armies of Bengal, Bombay and Madras, each with its own high command, staff and local Indian troops.

The headquarters of my father's unit was at Roorkee and the colonel had ordered him to go to Hardwar, about 40 miles away, to put a trestle bridge across the canal, for the convenience of the pilgrims. The bridging unit numbered on its strength six magnificent Indian elephants. They contributed the brawn and, one could almost say, the brains in bridging operations. The unit, with the elephants pulling large carts loaded with timber, lumbered along for four days before arriving at the site for the bridge on the far side of the canal, opposite Hardwar.

Among the numerous hangers-on in this caravan were two small boys, my brother Paul, aged two, and myself, aged three and a half. Our mother was also with us. Her name was Roberta. She was expecting a baby shortly and left us much to our own devices. We enjoyed three days of running wild up and down the canal bank, watching the elephants haul timber baulks about as if they were large matchsticks. We had picnic lunches, napped in the shade of trees and, when we awoke, clambered on to our *ayah*'s hips to be given forbidden sweetmeats.

Whilst the whole business of bridge-building seemed to us a delightful adventure, it was in fact tremendously hard work, involving a lot of skill on the part of those involved. In those days most improvised bridges were constructed of large timber trestles, the supporting pillars being huge baulks of timber resting upon similar baulks, the whole surmounted by a horizontal baulk supporting the wooden road itself. The whole contraption was held together by enormous iron spikes driven in by sledgehammers.

Paul and I watched the whole process until at last the moment came for launching the trestles into the canal, which was 70 feet wide at that point. The elephants seemed delighted to enter the water, their favourite element, whilst working. We watched them as the trestles were jockeyed into position, the cross timbers spiked and the timber decking secured.

Rani Leads the Way
The bridge looked good, standing some ten feet above the swiftly flowing water to allow for possible spates and a rise in

the water level. My father stood with arms akimbo admiring his work and that of his sappers and elephants. Pilgrims gathered on the banks gazing at the shortcut to Hardwar.

However, before any of them could set foot on the bridge my father decided upon a piece of showmanship, whether to demonstrate his faith in his handiwork or because he felt that his own family should be the first to cross the triumphal arch. Whatever his reason, he announced that Rani, the largest and heaviest of the elephants, should cross the bridge carrying the precious burden of his pregnant wife and two small sons.

'Robert, are you sure it's safe?' my mother asked apprehensively.[1]

'It looks so frail and that elephant must weigh at least five tons and from its back there will be a 20-foot drop.' My father laughed.

'It's as safe as houses. If I had the slightest doubt I would not risk your necks.'

Rani, obedient to the instructions of her *mahout*, knelt down calmly. Paul and I clambered excitedly on to the *howdah*, my mother following slowly and reluctantly.

Sitting on Rani's neck the *mahout* prodded her behind the ears with his big toes, the nails of which were sharpened to points. She rose gracefully and allowed herself to be directed on to the bridge.

---

1. The first names of George Roche's parents were Robert and Roberta. I noticed that, in the original typescript of this book, in all the records of direct speech between his parents, his father never addressed his mother by any name at all. That seemed unlikely, so I asked George about it. He said that both his parents addressed each other as 'Rob', which might confuse the reader. To avoid that he decided to omit her first name from all his attempts to record the direct speech of his father to his mother. I understand that George's brother Paul, referring to this matter, says that, when his parents called to each other in their various Indian homes, it was like listening to a couple of song birds. In this book I have followed George's solution to the problem. (RT)

Seated in the *howdah* on the huge elephant's back, we had a grandstand view of the multitude of pilgrims, the flag-be-decked town and the temples garishly decorated in blue and gold on the far side of the canal. Rani plodded on to the bridge waving her trunk from side to side, a recognized indication of nervousness, and perhaps the apprehensiveness of our mother was transmitting uneasy vibrations to Rani.

We crossed the first span, but as the weight of the elephant descended upon the trestle the timbers groaned and creaked, something fully expected.

When my mother heard it she cried out, 'Rob! Rob! The bridge is going to break and we shall all drown!

Her words panicked us, and her wail seemed frail compared to the high-pitched screams of Paul and myself.

The startled pilgrims started an instant clamour. Here was a fine start to the Mela, the sacrifice of a white *memsahib* and two small boys to the river goddess.

Nothing like it had happened before. Rani, prodded vigorously by the *mahout*, shuffled on till we reached the other side.[2]

We dismounted sobbing and shaking. My mother rushed to my father and let out a storm of highly effective language.

The more he expostulated about the safety of the bridge, the shriller became her protests, and they moved off arguing when our two *ayah*s came along, picked us up and cuddled us to their ample bosoms.

The pilgrims streamed across the bridge laughing and jostling, even if the goddess had been cheated of her sacrifice.

2. At a similar time of year in 1980 I crossed an almost identical trestle bridge of similar vintage over one of the tributaries of the Ganges in northern Bihar. When my car moved very slowly at least 60 feet above the swirling muddy stream the timbers of the bridge creaked alarmingly. An occasional elephant with its howdah and burdens can still be seen crossing the same bridges as in thepast. (RT)

High drama had been enacted and it had been a splendid show.

The terror of that incident is my earliest memory, unforgettable after so many decades.

2
England

'Get it out of the house, boy!' the fierce old gentleman with flashing eyes and bristling whiskers
shouted at me as I approached him with my dripping offering. My first meeting with my maternal grandfather
had coincided with my first sight of snow, lying in the driveway of Court Lodge, an Elizabethan house surrounded by a
high wall and situated in four acres of lawns and winter-bare
apple trees. It was at Gillingham, in Kent. In my excitement
about the strange white stuff I had scooped up handfuls of it
and borne it inside to show to my grandfather. He was the
colonel commandant of a famous infantry regiment, instilling
fear and meting out harsh discipline to the troops under his
command. He was irate to see snow melting into his Axmin-
ster carpet. Now, on my first visit to England, I watched
forlornly as my beautiful snowballs ran through my fingers,
leaving my hands empty and cold.[1]

1. The name of the fierce old gentleman was Lieutenant-Colonel Robert
Lewis Arathoon. He was born in Madras on 25 September, of Armenian
lineage. There were many Arathoons in India, especially in Madras and
Calcutta. All of them were the descendants of successive waves of
Christian refugees from persecution by Turkish and Persian Muslim
fanatics ever since the fourteenth century AD.
 At the India Office Library and Records in London there is a
considerable literature about the Armenians in India, their language, their

My parents and we children had just arrived from India on their first long leave since before the First World War, in the winter of 1918. Berths on ships just then were hard to come by. Because my mother had been seriously ill after giving birth to my sister Sylvia, the RAMC surgeon at Roorkee had somehow managed to obtain passages for us on an Australian hospital ship, the *Karula*. With hindsight it seems possible that her experience on the trestle bridge at Hardwar could have precipitated the birth.

Although not yet four years old at that time, I recall something of the voyage. The ship had a permanent list to port and seemed to be manned by a bevy of large, boot-faced women

arrivals and dispersions in the sub-continent, and I spent a whole day in an attempt to trace records of Colonel Arathoon's birth and family links. His birth in 1844 is quaintly recorded in the *Madras Almanack*, a massive commercial publication produced annually between 1806 and 1905: 'To the lady of John Arathoon Esq., a son.' No other Arathoon births are recorded for that year, but for the year 1846 there is a record of a marriage: 'At the Luz by the Revd Francisco de Dores, and afterwards at St George's Cathedral, by the venerable Archdeacon H. Harper, T. R. Holmes Esq., 49th NI, to Eliza, third daughter of John Arathoon Esq.' The capital letters 'NI' indicate that Holmes was a second or first lieutenant in the 49th battalion of the Madras Native Infantry.

In the time available I was not able to trace the name of Colonel Arathoon's mother. Neither the births nor the baptisms of Christians in India were compulsorily registrable, as they were in the UK. Judging by the military career of Colonel Arathoon, as fully recorded in the National Army Museum in London, all of which was served in the Northamptonshire Regiment, it seems that John Arathoon (whose vocation I was unable to trace) probably brought his entire family to England early in the lives of the children, of whom there must have been at least four. All this could probably be unravelled. A list of the sailings of vessels from Madras and Calcutta, giving the names of all the passengers on board, could be made, by scanning the pages of the main British or Indian newspapers of the epoch. That could be pretty time-consuming. In the years between 1840 and 1846, as recorded in the volumes of the *Madras Almanack* I consulted, I noticed that all six Arathoons whose names I found had purely English first names, not Armenian ones. This alone is of considerable interest. (RT) who terrified us. These gorgons, no doubt extremely worthy ladies, were Australian nurses whose merest glance produced instant obedience. Meals seemed to consist entirely of bowls of gruel administered by these females on one of the upper decks about noon daily. Perhaps adult passengers ate tastier meals in a dining room somewhere, but I have no recollection of seeing any such room. My father spent most of his time in our cramped cabin looking after my mother and the puling baby, Sylvia. Paul and I spent most of our time wandering about the ship with no supervision. One day when there was a very heavy sea running we reported on deck for the midday meal as usual, and a fierce nurse ordered us to sit with our backs against a bulkhead. As she handed us each a bowl of the mysterious gruel-cum-soup mixture, she barked, 'Eat it all up. You won't get anything else.'

Whilst we were forcing down this rather nauseating mixture, a large wave swept across the deck, knocking us both sideways. Being the heavier I did not travel far, but little Paul was swept into the scuppers, his bowl of gruel still clutched in his small hands. Just at that spot in the scuppers there was no deck rail and for several seconds my small brother teetered on the brink of going overboard. A passing seaman grabbed him, cursing and wondering what sort of parents could expose a tiny tot to such a risk. It was the most exciting moment of the whole voyage, of which I remember little else.

Court Lodge
On landing in England we went first to stay with my mother's parents at Court Lodge. It stood at the end of a cul-de-sac, opposite an ancient church, the peal of whose bells on Sundays was deafening. Next to the church was a footpath leading to the River Medway (or Mudway, as my mother described it).

Court Lodge, like most houses of the Tudor period, was full of nooks and crannies and little staircases. There seemed to be a staircase round every corner on every floor. Perhaps some of them were intended for the use of maids, but I never met any when exploring up and down them. Paul and I shared a bedroom, which must have been quite high up because from its windows we could see a long way across the countryside. The whole scene appeared to be constantly enveloped in grey mist. The cold mists of England made me long for the burning sun of India. Our bedroom, however, was made cosy and cheery by the fire, which burned in the grate all day, tended by a young girl whose name I thought to be Tweeny. Tweeny was supposed to 'give eye' to us. It seemed to us very strange to be put in the charge of a white girl who was no more than a child. We missed our motherly *ayah*s very much.

Lying in bed at night watching the flickering firelight on the ceiling, I imagined all sorts of creatures creeping about the silent house, so shut up and enclosed compared with the rambling bungalow in which we lived in India. My imaginings were made vivid by the fact that, down in the cellar, my mother had shown me a bricked-up trapdoor in the floor, which, she said, had once been the entrance to an underground passage leading from Court Lodge under the church and thence to the river. This provided a quick getaway for priests who said Mass in the house during the turbulent reign of Queen Elizabeth, when the celebration of Mass was a treasonable offence. Wide awake in my bed I imagined a figure coming along the passage, forcing open the trapdoor and making its way quietly upstairs.

There were a cook and a housemaid at Court Lodge as well as the little Tweeny,[2] who lit the bedroom fire. It seemed

2. The word 'tweeny' was short for 'between maid', a servant who combined the duties of assistant to the cook and housemaid. The expression was common in my own childhood, but was being replaced by the more general expression 'maid of all work'. A similar term was 'cook-general'. Such terms were used during the last few years before the virtual disappearance of domestic service in Britain during the late 1920s. (RT)

strange that in my grandfather's house the servants were white. I had never seen white ladies in that role before. They did not seem nearly so cheerful as our Indian servants, and the cook often rebuked us sharply when we went into her kitchen.

Woodside

It was different at Woodside, the house of my father's parents. This was a tall, narrow semi-detached house on the Uxbridge Road, in an outer suburban district of West London. Grandpa Roche was less forbidding than Grandpa Arathoon, and Grandma Roche and her sister, whom everyone called Tante, were kindly, loving souls, who took to their hearts the three small grandchildren they had never seen before.

My grandmother and Tante ran the three-storey house with the assistance of Jane, a maid of all work, who was more like one of the family than a servant. She was a cheerful woman, very kind to us children, and our longing for our *ayah*s began to recede.

At this time of our lives, like most small children of British parents in India, Paul and I could speak little English. Our mother's health, moreover, had been poor for a long time, so that our lives had been spent largely with our *ayah*s, the other servants in the compound, and with their children. We spoke Urdu much better than our mother tongue. We often spoke to each other, or replied to remarks addressed to us, in Urdu, which had the gratifying effect of making Jane marvel at our ability actually to speak a foreign language.

However, Grandma and Tante thought that I, at least, should be able to speak more English, and tried to encourage me by speaking slowly and clearly whenever they addressed me. 'This glass of milk is for you, Georgie', Grandma would say as she put it in front of me, or 'Here is a book for you to look at, Georgie', or 'Georgie. Pass the salt, please.'

My little brother followed me about like a shadow. Whenever he heard something being offered to Georgie he was so anxious not to be left out that he would pipe up '*Hum bi*' (Me too) at the sound of my name. Much amused, my Grandma dubbed him 'Humbi', and Humbi he remained to all the family for a very long time. Only recently, Humbi came over from America to visit us. We had not met for 25 years, but neither of us had forgotten how he came by his nickname.

Even in 1919 the Uxbridge Road was a busy thoroughfare, with trams clanging their way to the Uxbridge terminus some eight miles away. Despite the trams on their ribbons of rail, the setting of Woodside, compared with its appearance today, was rural onwards towards Oxford. The Uxbridge Road was bounded on either side by orchards and market gardens.

My brother and I slept in the topmost bedroom of this five-bedroomed house. At night, the lights of the trams and flashes as the trolley poles collected electricity from the overhead cables would make fascinating patterns on the ceiling as we dropped off to sleep. Patterns on ceilings in rooms high up, whether produced by fires in grates or sparks from trolley poles on tram routes, were novelties we had not known in India. They compensated somewhat for the absence of pulsating life in crowded bazaars and the sounds of the muezzin at dawn.

Everything about England was new to us and it was bewildering to discover that England was home. It was strange never to see a brown face when one went out.[3] The pave-

3. Despite the increasing longevity of most communities in the world, most people become so familiar with the general appearance of the public in our streets as to forget what they looked like a few decades ago. In these pages George is recalling a time when the sight of anybody of African, Indic or Far Eastern appearance was a rarity anywhere in Britain, despite the global extent of the former imperial domain. Large-scale immigration from former colonial territories did not begin until after the Second World War, and was largely a constitutional consequence of the process of decolonization. Although the political leaders of nationalist movements demanded both 'self-government' and 'independence', neither could be

ments of Oxford Street were as crowded as those of Bombay, but everyone was white. It was strange to ride on a tram or in a train that went underground; even stranger to ride in a hansom cab, with a white driver sitting at the back, instead of in a *tonga* with an Indian driver sitting in front.

Motorcars we knew about. Some of my father's friends had them in India, and my father had a motorcycle appropriately called an 'Indian', and often took us for rides in the big wickerwork sidecar. I wished very much that the motorcycle was at Woodside, and that we could use it to explore the countryside. We could have gone much further afield than was possible in a tram or on foot.

Hats and Nice New Suits

My mother delighted in going to Harrods to shop. Although I had enjoyed going shopping with her to the bazaars in India in the pony trap, I did not really care very much for going to Harrods. It involved a ride in a tram to Ealing Common and a journey by underground to Knightsbridge. Harrods was dull and the white assistants seemed very aloof and indifferent to customers, compared to the volatile, friendly traders, bartering volubly in the bazaars.

Paul and Sylvia were usually left behind in the care of Grandma and Jane when my mother took me to Harrods. I now know that she would have preferred to have left me behind too. But she decided that two small boys and a baby girl would be too onerous for her mother-in-law. It puzzled me one day when she brought Paul shopping with us.

I do not know which of the department stores had the privilege of attending to our requirements that day. Anyway, we were made to try on endless pairs of silky white trousers and

legally provided for unless the possessors of the new nationalities were given the right to come to Britain if they chose to do so. Had such rights not been included in the constitutions of the territories concerned, the process of decolonization would have been delayed interminably. (RT) silky white jackets, some with lace collars, until my mother was perfectly satisfied and we were perfectly horrified.

After a short break for cakes and tea in the store's tearoom, we accompanied our mother to the millinery department, a torture chamber for us, a paradise for herself.

She tried on hat after hat, whilst we sat on a small sofa in a corner and eyed the disembodied heads sporting the latest headgear that were stood about on counters.

'You bought two hats!' we heard our father exclaim soon after we had returned from the expedition.

'Well, I couldn't decide which I liked best,' my mother replied.

'And I thought I'd see which one you liked best.'

They were talking quite loudly in their bedroom and the door was open, so it was easy to hear my father grunt in reply.

'Look,' my mother said. 'What about this one?'

'Mmm. Very nice,' said father.

'And this one?' mother asked.

'Mmm. That's nice too.'

'Oh Rob,' she said exasperatedly: 'You want me to look my best don't you? Everyone will be looking at us, you know, and I don't want them to think I've got old-fashioned since I've been in India.'

My heart sank. Everyone was going to be looking at us, were they, and we were going to be wearing awful white silk suits.

'Aren't they lovely?' my mother was saying.

Through the open door we could see her lifting them out of their tissue-paper wrappings.

We did not like the way we looked in our nice new suits, but we were dressed in them and waiting for our mother to stop changing her hats.

Grandma and Tante were resplendent in their Sunday best hats. Grandpa was sedate in a somewhat old-fashioned suit of good quality, and my father was elegant in an expensive new suit chosen by our mother. 'After all, you are the best man,' she had insisted, when he demurred at the expense.

We were going to a wedding. Our father's brother, introduced to us as our Uncle Lawrence only a few days before, was getting married. All eyes that were not upon the bride would be upon the family of the groom, particularly members from India who had never been seen by the bride's family and friends.

My mother had finally settled for the floppy hat with the roses on it, and when she joined us in the hallway I thought she looked beautiful. My father looked at her as though he thought so too. Grandpa opened the front door. The hired car was at the kerb. We went and seated ourselves in it.

The wedding itself has long since melded into the images of the many other weddings I have since attended, but the memory of the reception remains distinct. Green lawns, shady trees, a bright marquee and lots of delicious food. I do not know why the food should have impressed me so much, because I cannot remember any specific dishes, apart from ice cream (which I do not think I had ever tasted before) and wonderful cakes.

I also remember a lot of pretty little girls being rather nice to me. Some were the bride's sisters, and one of them was not much older than I was. The bride herself was only 19. They were now my sisters-in-law, and perhaps they felt solicitous towards me. Hindsight tells me that, most likely, they were also curious about me.

The reception was being held in their large and beautiful garden, and the girls took me round it, telling me the names of shrubs and bushes because 'Coming from India you won't know anything about English gardens at all.' They were right. England was an impression: India reality.

15

My father's leave drew to a close and he returned to India alone. My mother's health was such that the doctor advised her to remain in England until she was much stronger before she made the long journey.

When our mother was at last fit to travel, it was discovered that our baby sister was not strong and might not live if she were to accompany us back to India. It was decided that she should be left behind at Woodside with our grandparents until she was older and stronger she was older and stronger.[4]

4. The above paragraphs, and many other passages in this book, illustrate one of the most characterstic features of British family life associated with the tropical world of India, most of Africa, the Caribbean and parts of Latin America since the last few decades of the nineteenth century. Virtually all concerned with it, in all branches of the public service and private sector, became aware of the separation of husbands and wives, parents and children, enduring for decade after decade, deeply affecting the British educational structure in its middle and upper strata, and the home lives of large sections of the population. Similar problems were experienced by other imperial powers. The British and other Protestant dominated powers tended to support racial separation. The Latin and Roman Catholic powers tended to support intermarriage with the people of dependent countries, which avoided the separation of men, women, parents and children. (RT)

3
Back to India:
SS *Dufferin*

One summer's day in 1919 we travelled to Tilbury docks and boarded the SS *Dufferin*, a smallish ship, sparkling white, all her brass fittings gleaming in the sun. It was this ship that later took the Prince of Wales (later King Edward VIII) to India and provided the first stage of a generally successful flag show. Some of his appearances in areas dominated by Gandhi's supporters were marred by Congress toughs, but more of that later.

The SS *Dufferin* was an attractive ship and we had a much more enjoyable voyage aboard her than we had had on the *Karula*. Once again Paul and I spent much of our time exploring the decks whilst our mother sat sunning herself in a deck chair, reading or chatting with other passengers. When it was time for children's meals she took us into the dining room and supervised us. There were quite a few children on board, and some were allowed to take their meals without any supervision by parents. We stared at them wonderingly, for they seemed to play about most of the time and to talk with their mouths full. Sometimes they even got down from their chairs and left the table before they had eaten everything on their plates.

Whilst our mother rested in the afternoons, we toured all the passenger accommodation. The lower decks had cabins on both sides of long passageways. Sometimes we encountered sinister creatures scuttling along with us — bold, self-assured rats. Like all ships in those days, the SS *Dufferin* harboured dozens of rats in her bowels. They could often be seen brazenly cleaning their whiskers, as if asserting their right to be aboard. Though interested in watching them, I was unprepared for the fright one of them was soon to give me.

One night I was sleeping peacefully in my bunk when I became aware of something on my face. I awoke with horror to find a rat staring into my eyes. This nightmarish event had a sequel. A few nights later, when my mother came into the cabin after dinner to see that all was well with her little sons, she gently caressed my face. I shrieked out, sat bolt upright and began beating away my mother's hand and sobbing uncontrollably. It was some time before I could explain to her the reason for my strange behaviour.

The voyage was otherwise uneventful, but at dusk there was always a scary feeling that there might still be submarines lurking in the darkening sea, and there was a very real fear of loose-floating mines that were known to be about so soon after the war. These posed a danger to all shipping.

The danger was brought home to us when we stopped at Marseilles, and mother took us for a walk along the quay to show us a ship that had struck a mine. There was a huge hole in her side, which was being stopped by a gang of men pouring endless buckets of cement against some sort of shuttering. The sight had a great impact on us; after we left Marseilles we gazed out to sea watching for the horned monsters that could cause such devastation to a ship at sea.

As the days went by and we approached closer to Port Said the very atmosphere changed subtly. The West was disappearing and the East taking over. This was my first experience of a feeling to be repeated over and over again whenever I neared

18

Back to India: *SS* Dufferin

Port Said at the end of the Mediterranean: I was going home.

Arrival

India. Bombay. The *Dufferin* had docked. Bombay had appeared out of the heat haze of early morning, and Paul and I hung over the rail of the upper deck looking to see if our father was among the great mass of bodies on the quayside. In those days, long before terrorist activities had caused docks to be cordoned off for the protection of passengers, ships and cargoes, the quays were crowded with brown-skinned dock workers, together with freelance porters known as 'coolies'. They swarmed up the gangplanks to board the ships, to grab for luggage to carry ashore.

Our father was there, standing somewhat aloof, his topi shading his face and the back of his neck as he waited for us to disembark. We flung ourselves at him and he picked us up one after the other to give us a hug, before greeting our mother with a chaste kiss on the brow. It was not done to make public displays of affection, and my mother would have been embarrassed had my father hugged her as he had hugged us. Just outside the dock area my father hired one of the waiting victorias and we all got inside the large, horse-drawn cab and were driven into town.[1]

Early as it was, the city was pulsating with life. The beggars who slept on the pavements had awoken, blinked their eyes and defecated in the gutters. With begging bowls and scrawny hands they were already soliciting for coins. The noise was cacophonous — a never-ending honking of hooters, the creakings and groanings of cart wheels, puffings and snortings of animals pulling a variety of vehicles, the sounds of cattle bells, the cries of hawkers, shrill voices raised in argument or

1. These large, very old-fashioned vehicles, looking extremely battered with age, could still be seen in Bombay in 1980, but they did not seem to collect many passengers, apart from a few sentimental Europeans or larking young Indians. (RT)

in bartering. There were the sounds of coughing and spitting as old men cleared their throats and spat on the pavements, of children crying or shrieking as they chased each other, unseen women wailing for reasons we would never know, piping reedy music coming from dark alleyways. In those days there were no transistor radios and, unseen, the musician would be sitting crossed-legged with his reed pipe or flute at his lips.

A great mass of humanity and animals swarmed about the victoria. All around us there were goats and donkeys, bullock carts, wandering cattle, rotting garbage in the gutters, steaming pats of fresh cow dung, charcoal braziers, burnt fat, spicy and acrid smells, and flies on everything. These were the smells and the sights we were used to. We breathed contentedly, and knew that, at last, we were home.

My father, a civilian again, was now district manager of the large network of the Great Indian Peninsular Railway (the GIP) in the Deccan, with his headquarters at Sholapur. We were going to travel there from Bombay by train, but it was not due to leave until evening. We had all day to wait.

My mother decided that part of the time available could be spent very nicely shopping in Whiteway & Laidlaw's, the large department store which catered almost exclusively for Europeans and which, by means of three-bladed electric fans twirling slowly from the ceilings, offered a cooler atmosphere for browsing than that of the stifling bazaars in the streets. We did not actually need anything. My mother had arranged for Paul and me to be properly kitted out at the Army & Navy Stores in London, and she had updated her own wardrobe with new lingerie, formal and informal dresses, large-brimmed hats and elbow-length gloves to wear at the functions and garden parties that lay ahead of us. Still, with time to kill she soon had us trying on little khaki shorts and shirts and open sandals that could be useful supplements to our own wardrobes.

The shop assistants were pretty Eurasian girls noted for their

20

charm, and the way they fussed around us was very different from the disdainful attention given to us by the white assistants at Harrods. These soft-eyed girls pulled out endless garments from stacked drawers. As they held them up against us, they smiled and told us in their soft voices how well each garment would suit us.

My father soon tired of all this and, in reply my mother's question: 'But what else can we do?' replied: 'We can take the boys to Crawford Market. It will be a treat for them.'

Squawks, Birds and Bananas

The Crawford Market was famous for exotic birds and small, rare animals of every description were on display there. Dozens of varieties of parrots, from large cockatoos to common parakeets were screeching all round us. The small, rare animals seemed to be represented only by marmosets and vervet monkeys, but there were a great number of them.

My father promised to buy a bird each for us, provided we chose ones that were not too expensive. Paul, however, had his heart set on a marmoset, and pleaded so eloquently for it that he might have succeeded had it not been so pricey. He was told to forget it and choose a bird. Eventually he settled for a small green parrot, very common all over India, and cheap. He called it Polly Perkins at my mother's suggestion.

I chose a hill mynah with large yellow wattles under its beak. The Indian dealer said it could speak fluently in Urdu and English. It never uttered a single word. All it would do after my efforts to teach it to repeat a few words after me was utter a loud squawk when it wanted a banana. It could eat a hand of bananas a day. As fast as a banana went in at one end it came out the other.

I called my mynah George, in the hope that those who heard him would think he was trying to attract my attention. My mother, with her tongue in her cheek, referred to him as George Minor. At the time her joke escaped me, and it was

21

only much later that I realized that, at the time my father bought the mynah, I shared with it a passion for bananas.

Our purchases safely in their cages, and the cages grasped firmly in our hot little hands, we allowed our parents to drag us away from Crawford Market and to a taxi, which trundled us along to Victoria Station. There, in a siding, stood my father's special railway coach and some of our servants, awaiting us.

As soon as they saw us they expressed great joy at being reunited with us, exclaiming in amazement about how tall and handsome we had grown. Their praises were so fulsome that we felt embarrassed and stood dumbly as they chattered.

Lela, my *ayah*, put her arms about Paul and me, whilst Ahmed Khan, our bearer, greeted my mother gravely, bewailing her long absence. She responded by expressing her pleasure in being back home again. Yusuf, our cook, paid his respects to her. Then the whole ritual of greeting us was repeated.[2]

Ahmed and Yusuf then went to their quarters in the coach, and Lela began to get us ready for our supper, washing our hands and faces in the hand basin that stood in the compartment leading off the bedroom, and then combed our hair.

The coach was well-equipped. As district manager of the GIP, my father was often required to inspect miles of the existing railway lines and to oversee the laying of new ones.

---

2. This memory of greetings is significant. There is much evidence that the peoples of tropical countries, especially those of the Indian subcontinent, are far more sensitive, volatile and effusive about human relationships than those of northern Europe, and especially of Britain. My father, himself an exceptionally emotional European, believed that, whatever the merits of his colleagues as rulers of the Raj, their greatest weakness was their cold indifference to the emotional warmth of their subjects. He was convinced, already in the late 1920s, soon after his own arrival in Bihar, that the Indian Empire was doomed for this reason alone. (RT)

The coach enabled him to travel extensively on duty. Completely self-contained with a dining room, bedroom en suite, kitchen and a separate compartment for servants, it could be attached to any train and towed along behind it.

We were soon to be shunted on to the rear of the *Deccan Queen*, the express that would take us to Sholapur 500 miles away.

When the great train pulled out Paul and I were supping on biscuits and milk given to us by Lela. The station and its lights receded and we plunged into the darkness of the countryside. Lela undressed us, put us into our pyjamas and lifted us into our bunks. Paul's was over my father's bunk and mine over my mother's. We were asleep in seconds. When we awoke the pink fingers of dawn were probing the grassy plains of the Deccan.

4

Sholapur

We breakfasted on bananas and tea, George Minor squawking until I pushed a piece of my banana between the bars of his cage. It was then that I discovered his passion for them. I was unwilling to go more than 50:50 with him, and he continued to voice his disapproval of what he considered my unfairness long after all the bananas were finished.

Fortunately we were able to buy more when the train stopped at the next station. There were then no restaurant cars on Indian trains. When a train stopped at a major station approximately at a meal time, it halted for an hour or so to enable passengers to take meals at various restaurants on the platform, some more luxurious than others, and intended for people of differing religions and castes. At many stations, too, passengers could replenish such supplies of food as they carried with them.[1]

1. Today the position has changed. Platform restaurants have almost disappeared. At large stations the catering staff on a train collect containers of cooked food, which are kept hot in a special compartment of the train. Waiters visit the first- and second-class compartments and make lists of the dishes requested by passengers. In 1980 I found such arrangements less enjoyable than those of 40 years earlier. Whilst journeys occupied less time, the trays of food became tepid in transit through long, crowded corridors in the trains. (RT)

In our coach Yusuf was able to prepare curry and rice for us for lunch and supper, but we found that we had to buy bananas for George Minor whenever we saw them for sale on a station platform.

Stops at stations were numerous on our journey. Third-class passengers lacked adequate toilet facilities in their coaches and took advantage of stops to relieve themselves all over the railway lines and embankments near the stations.

The windows of our coach commanded an excellent view of such proceedings, the like of which we had not encountered on the Ealing line, until our mother snapped down the window blinds.

It was evening when the *Deccan Queen* puffed in to Sholapur. We had been travelling for about 24 hours, and were tired and anxious to get home to our bungalow.

The Bungalow
Our bungalow was a large L-shaped building under thatch, with a wide verandah all round it. One arm of the L contained the bedrooms and bathrooms. The other contained the sitting and dining rooms. The back door of the dining room led by a covered pathway to the kitchen.

All the floors were laid with thick blocks of a locally mined stone called *sharbad*, and my parents had strewn them with Indian and Persian rugs.

Basic furniture was supplied by the railway company: wicker armchairs, a teak dining table and chairs, teak beds, wardrobes and dressing tables, all of which gave the bungalow a Victorian appearance inside.

The curtains and all the silver, cutlery, crockery, ornaments and pictures were our own. It was a joy to see everything again, arranged just as it had been in our bungalow at Roorkee before we went on leave.

My mother was most pleased with the way everything looked and complimented Ahmed on his achievement. In her absence, he had supervised everything just as she would have done herself.[2]

Mina, my brother's *ayah*, was expressing her delight at seeing her 'Baba Sahib' again, clasping him to her chest, kissing his curls and holding him at arm's length to admire his height and beauty. And she admired his common green parrot when he showed it to her, bursting with the pride of ownership. Then she carried him off to one of the bathrooms to give him a bath and wash his golden hair, tousled by the train journey.

Lela, not to be outdone, fussed around me and took me to see my new bedroom, beaming with pleasure as she showed me my bed, which she had chosen for me as the more comfortable of the two in the room.

Lela considered that the first-born in a family was of greater

2. Throughout India and the whole British colonial world, housing arrangements for all middle and senior-ranking officers of government, and for the similar staff of important companies and other organizations, both indigenous and British, were not unlike those of George Roche's parents at Sholapur. Houses and basic furniture were supplied by the organizations concerned and graded in size and quality for personnel of varied status. Such things as bed linen, blankets, carpets and tableware belonged to the staff. This was satisfactory during most of the years of an officer's service, when personal mobility was essential to enable him or her to be posted from one district to another, or from one territory to another, or to be moved on promotion. It had serious personal drawbacks, however. On his first appointment, say, from Britain, an officer had to purchase a large quantity of household goods to take overseas to equip the 'residence' to which he would be allocated. Since he would not receive his first payment of salary for many weeks, he usually had to borrow a considerable sum. And, well before he retired on pension, he had somehow to acquire a house or flat of his own in Britain or elsewhere. The last problem caused serious worries for many staff at times of their lives when their official responsibilities were at their greatest. The problem was conducive to an unfortunate mutual estrangement between many officers and the indigenous peoples among whom they had worked during their official lives. (RT)

importance than any subsequent children. I took precedence over Paul, and she took precedence over Mina.

We supped on biscuits and milk, sitting on the sides of our beds with our *ayah*s in attendance. When we had finished we scrambled into bed and Mina and Lela took our trays away. Soon our mother came in to kiss us goodnight. She looked tired, for she had not slept well on the train and as soon as we arrived at the bungalow she had begun to supervise the servants whilst they unpacked the trunks containing the new household goods that had been bought in London; and now she was in the midst of unpacking her own suitcases.

She and my father would eat only a quick snack for supper because my mother would not rest until she had everything shipshape for the morning, when the daily routine of our life at Sholapur would begin.

The Maratha Stronghold

Sholapur was in the heart of the Deccan, set square in the old Maratha stronghold. The town was nondescript, with the usual bazaar where most of the Indian population lived, and there was a small cantonment for two companies of a British regiment.

Cotton of fairly high quality was grown in the area, and cotton mills had sprung up to process it into durable, if rather coarse, material. Later we were to appreciate how durable the cotton goods were. Our towels and sheets of Sholapur cotton lasted us boys right through our three years of prep school in England, and well into our days at Ushaw College. They never wore out and we became sick of the sight of them.

The Marathas were a light-boned, but very tough and sinewy people, noted for their military keenness and readiness for a fight. The Indian Army recruited many of them and they formed some fine regiments which did well in the 1914–18 war and achieved even more in the second great war to come.

During the Indian Mutiny of 1857/8 (known today as 'the

Uprising') their relations with the British Raj had been hostile, which explains the existence of the small British garrison at Sholapur thereafter.

At this time Mahatma Gandhi had found many keen supporters for his 'Free India' campaign among the Marathas working in the cotton mills, and I remember an incident that illustrates this.

A Taste of Non-Violence

One day, after we had been for a picnic on the bank of the Bhima River, which flowed about seven miles from the town, we were driving along the road home in the 'Indian' motor-bike and sidecar when, to our consternation, we saw on the road ahead a large concourse of Gandhi Congress *wallahs*, distinguished by their small coarse cotton pillbox hats, hand-woven to symbolize their allegiance to the cause of Indian freedom from the accursed British oppressors. There was no means of escape. The road ahead had to be taken through the crowd.

My father drove cautiously. As we approached the crowd he told us to crouch down as low as we could into the sidecar, which we did. As we moved into the crowd milling all over the road, curses and insults were screamed at us; stones were hurled and sticks whacked on the motorbike, the sidecar and my father's back. He reacted to the assault by opening the motorbike's silencer (by pulling a lever the silencer could be cut out completely). The full roar of the massive two cylinders rent the air. At the same time my father opened the throttle to its full extent and we surged through the crowd which parted suddenly, scattering to the sides of the road.

Luckily no great harm had been done and we returned home intact, my mother pale and shaken. Paul and I were full of excitement as we babbled out the adventure to Mina and Lela, whose eyes grew round with horror at the danger we had escaped.

Our mother told us that our experience should be considered not exciting, but fearsome. She was steeped in horror tales about the Mutiny of the past, and could easily imagine a similar uprising at any time. If my father had not kept his head and taken advantage of the element of surprise caused by releasing the silencer to startle the crowd, allowing him to speed through, we might have been forced to slow down and stop, perhaps even topple over, and been seriously assaulted. 'Non-violence can turn into mob violence in seconds,' my mother said. 'When you say your prayers tonight, pray that we never meet a crowd like that again.'

The station at Sholapur, on the main line south from Bombay to Madras, was a junction for branch lines running east to Hyderabad and west to Kolapur.

My father was the district engineer responsible for the maintenance of these lines and their extension. He was assisted by two European resident engineers.

He and his assistants were professional officers on the staff of the Great Indian Peninsular Railway (GIP) and their office was about half a mile from the station itself.

The GIP employed a great many workers on its stations and trains. They were Eurasians and Indians. In India as a whole, the Eurasian community tended to be concentrated in vocations that would not have developed at all in rural India had it not been for the historical links with the West, such as rail transport, the post and telegraph services and a great deal of office work, in both the private and the public sectors.

The Eurasians lived apart from both the European and the Indian communities. This did not seem strange to me as a child, and I was quite unaware that they were people of mixed descent. Nor did I know that a great many Indians wanted to see the back of the Europeans.

My father, an engineer who built the bridges and railways which have served the whole sub-continent ever since, providing the lifelines of industry and commerce, considered himself and his colleagues to be more useful to India than the collectors (district magistrates, both administrative and judicial), but this was an opinion he voiced only to my mother in the privacy of our bungalow.

There we lived a life removed from the realities plaguing India. It was a halcyon time for small boys who did not have to worry about anything.

Chota Hazri, *Rides before Breakfast, Eggs and Snakes*

Paul and I would start the day as soon as it was light with a *chota hazri* (small breakfast) of tea with some fingers of buttered toast and a banana, brought to us by our *ayah*s from the kitchen. We would then dress for our morning ride, and the *syce* (groom) would lead round our two steeds. Mine was a horse called Rudolf, Paul's a very small mare, a pony called Tansy.

The *syce* would put Paul into a ring saddle from which it was impossible for him to fall. He did not like riding. He always felt very sorry for his pony, imagining that to pull on the reins would split its mouth. When he tried to direct the pony for a turn, he held the reins out as far as he could on either side. My father would shout at him to stop 'selling lace', because he looked as if he was in a haberdashery, measuring out yards of trimming. He never became a horseman, even in later years. His sensitive and kindly nature would not let him use the whip, and he could not even bring himself to jab his pony's sides with his little heels. His pony lagged behind with a lethargic gait.

Rudolf, my horse, was given to displays of tantrums. He once gave me a nasty kick in the chest as I approached him to mount. He bolted several times and once he threw me into a bed of cactus; I was picking cactus spikes out of my behind for weeks. When he bolted I used to cling to my saddle (a proper one) and hope for the best. Rudolf was tried out in my mother's trap a couple of times, but after the second attempt,

31

when he kicked the dashboard to pieces, he seldom had to suffer the indignity of having to pull it.

After our morning ride we would come home to a proper breakfast with our parents.[3] This usually consisted of a boiled egg and bread and butter cut into fingers for dipping into the egg.

The eggs were laid by our own hens, which had a large run in the compound. At night they lived in a small timber henhouse. It was our job to collect the eggs, and one day to our horror we found a large cobra enjoying a couple of eggs in the henhouse. Cries of alarm brought our mother with her 12-bore gun. She let fly with No 5 shot, which soon put an end to the cobra.

We were accustomed to snakes, of which there were quite a number in the compound, and we learnt quickly to distinguish the poisonous ones. However, on one occasion we found some beautiful tiny snakes with bright emerald patterns on their backs. We put two or three of these babies into our pockets and took them into the house, eager to show our mother the pretty new pets we had discovered. Horrified, she ordered Ahmed to kill them. 'You silly boys. Those are Russell's vipers, which are extremely poisonous, even when still so small.'

3. British memoirs of life in India contain many accounts of riding before breakfast as a daily routine. Apart from the fleeting beauty of the early morning scene, it afforded an opportunity for exercise in a climate not always conducive to it. It was greatly facilitated by the nature of the terrain.

Until the arrival of the road-building Europeans, wagons, camels, horses, donkeys and mules, used for transport of all kinds, moved only along earthen tracks, often obstructed by mud or deep ruts. The construction of all-weather roads provided new links between the major towns and markets, but still left wide stretches of land as open as they had been before, with areas suitable for riding or movement on foot between the patches of cultivation. Many Indians today are keen horsemen. (RT)

Vipers, unlike most snakes, which are hatched from eggs, are born directly from the bodies of their mothers, a considerable number at a single birth. Those we had found had been born quite recently but, young as they were, they would have been perfectly capable of biting us. Perhaps the tender way we had handled them had put them at ease.

The most dreaded snake was the king cobra, or *hamadryad*, which will attack on sight without provocation. Another deadly one is the krait, which grows to over a foot in length. It has a nasty habit of lying along roof beams and falling off, probably whilst asleep. Waking suddenly from such a fall in a bad temper, it strikes out at any moving thing near to it.

The krait has a sinister black skin with small speckles along its back, and we called it the 'bogey-man snake'. In those days there were no anti-snakebite serums. The usual treatment for snakebite was to place a tourniquet above the bite, cut into it with a sharp knife and, if you could, get someone to suck the bite and spit out the venom. This gave some chance of survival.

But if there was no handy 'sucker' about, the usual treatment was to rub in plenty of crystals of potassium permanganate and live in hope.

Our little fox terrier Lucy once attacked a cobra on the front lawn and got bitten on the lip. My father used the cut-and-rub method, applying plenty of crystals. The dog was very ill for a few days, but survived.

Corn Cobs in the Compound

On most of our mornings Paul and I were free to wander around the compound, talking to the servants, often going into their quarters and being given hot, sweet tea.

Sometimes we roasted corn or millet cobs on the hot embers of the fires that seemed to burn outside every hut, and would squat down and chat with the occupants of the huts as we

33

crunched these delicious morsels. No wonder we were not always very hungry at lunch time.

Sheep's Head Broth

Lunch was often something of an ordeal. My mother was a great believer in the goodness of sheep's head broth, with barley, rice and other vegetables thrown in. The taste was fine but the sight of bits of sheep's lips, or what seemed to be recognizable bits of its head, was enough to put one off, and in any case the sheep was probably a goat.

Billy Goats, Matings and Birth about us

Large herds of goats roamed the fields around Sholapur, usually tended by a *chokra*, a young goat herd. One often saw a large billy goat in a herd with a little leather apron round his waist. When we asked what the apron was for, the grown ups would quickly change the subject.

Their attempts to evade the subject of sex whetted our curiosity, and for many days we would follow the herds to discover the answer to our question. We found that a billy goat, attracted by a female in season, would be frustrated in the consummation of his desire by the leather apron. It provided a primitive form of birth control applied by the herd owner, possibly for selective breeding, or to give the nanny goats a breather from the continual rearing of kids.

At that time we ran about free from any educational restraints, learning from the natural things about us. We watched with fascination butterflies emerging from their chrysalises, the flight of white ants as they sped from their holes during the monsoon before falling wingless to the earth, to engage in 'follow my leader' pursuit by the males of the females over the lawns, looking for holes suitable for mating.

We watched the matings of dogs, horses and birds, learning the nature of male and female, and the purpose of their performance. The birth of puppies and foals held no mysteries for us.

The matings of horses, despite the attempts of our parents to deprive us of a grandstand view, were always intriguing events. The mare would play 'hard to get', kicking her heels, whinnying, snorting and dashing around the paddock chased by the persistent stallion, until at last she quietened down and allowed herself to be mounted.

Many years later when I was in the army, an old cavalry officer used to describe any slipshod drilling manoeuvres by recruits thus: 'What a laughy, kicky, farty way of doing things you lot have got!' I once asked him the precise meaning of his comment. He smiled and asked me if I had ever seen a mare being served. This at once reminded me of our life at Sholapur.

Heralds of the Monsoon

Sholapur was on a plateau about 1000 feet above sea level. Although the climate was hot, it was not as hot as the central and northern parts of India. The winter was milder than in northern India. Apart from the monsoon months,[4] the climate was dry and the grassy plains, with their strange small hills dotted about, were burnt brown for most of the year.

We arrived at Sholapur just before the monsoon. It was getting oppressively hot, with temperatures ranging from about 90 degrees Fahrenheit to about 113 degrees at midday. We found it intensely hot out of doors though, with our topis to protect us from sunstroke, we would have ventured out like the mad dogs and Englishmen created by Noel Coward, had our mother not forbidden us to do so. She told us to play quietly indoors.

Each sultry day was followed by the next. Every morning

---

4. The monsoon months extend between about the end of the first week of June and about mid-October. (RT)

the inhabitants would scan the distant mountains of the Western Ghats to see if clouds, heralds of the monsoon, were forming over them. Many days went by before the morning when a distant thunderhead appeared, and that had vanished by midday. But each day the clouds, massing high, became denser and started to move towards the plateau.

One very oppressive afternoon when my mother was lying on her bed with another of the headaches that affected her before the monsoon, we heard distant peals of thunder and could see lightning flashing from cloud to cloud.

My mother said that this was harmless sheet lightning, unlike the dreaded fork lightning, which could cause thunderbolts and strike one dead.

Then a few drops of rain fell, followed by larger drops, splashing on to the dry earth and sending up little spurts of dust. A glorious smell of wet earth came wafting over the plain and suddenly a torrential downpour spilled out of the black clouds, causing rivulets of muddy water into which huge raindrops splashed and rebounded, making us think of little frogs jumping for joy.

The whole family, including my mother, whose headaches were always cured as soon as torrential rain fell, ran outside into the downpour. The servants were already outside and we joined them, letting the rain stream down all over us. Soaked to the skin in seconds, we rejoiced after the heat of a few hours before. A fresh wind made it feel quite chilly, with the sudden drop in temperature of nearly 20 degrees.

At last the nights were bearable under our mosquito nets, which we had to use throughout the year, and we sighed with delight as we pulled up a light blanket over the sheet which had been our sole covering at night during the past weeks.

Now the monsoon was into its swing and for days at a stretch the rain teemed down. Sometimes it was irksome to be confined indoors, but the hot weather was over and no-one complained.

Forked Lightning

One afternoon a fearsome storm swept over the town, and the Railway Institute was struck by forked lightning. My father, who went to inspect the damage, said it had been caused by a thunderbolt and, unfortunately, three Eurasian clerks had been killed.

Our mother impressed upon us the danger of being outside when forked lightning was on display, and after that we became suitably alarmed whenever a storm approached.

Mother also expressed fears about the thatched roof, lest it should be struck by lightning and set on fire, but my father pooh-poohed this, arguing that there could be no danger of fire when the thatch was soaked in rainwater. When my mother asked what might happen if lightning struck just as the rain was beginning, he dismissed this as being extremely unlikely.

Nightmares and Ghosts

Anxiety raised by overhearing their conversation remained with me for some time. As I lay in bed at night, staring up through my mosquito net at the cloth ceiling high above,[5] I would imagine the roof bursting into flames, the cloth whirling up, to be followed by my mosquito net, and then the blazing lot falling down upon me.

The cloth ceiling provided a variety of chills to the spine, at the best of times. Not solid, it moved when any little creature scuttled about in the roof, making indentations in the cloth as it did so. Such effects were caused mainly by mice, but sometimes, in a breeze, the cloth would spring up and down like a trampoline. Sometimes I thought I could discern a trough

5. Cloth ceilings were common and are still in use. They resemble the inside of the roof of a tent suspended beneath the rafters or beneath beams and thatch, serving to protect the room below from miscellaneous droppings, living or otherwise. Such ceilings tend rapidly to become grey or stained, especially during the monsoon. (RT)

moving slowly across the ceiling. It could be caused by a snake, for there certainly were some in the roof. They could be slithering along in pursuit of mice for supper.

Draughts would ripple the ceiling cloth, and shadows thrown upon it by bright flashes of lightning appeared to move menacingly, even to reach down to grab a small boy. The mosquito net, too, had the effect of a distorting mirror when lit only by lightning and swayed by the breeze. The net curtains were like ghosts hovering about my bedside.

In the morning all was different and the room again a safe and friendly place, the fantasies of the night before only interesting subjects to describe to Paul, who did enjoy listening before our *ayah*s brought us our *chota hazri*. But the following night he refused to allow the lamp to be put out after we had been put to bed, and Mina soon found out why.

Next morning my mother reprimanded me for frightening my little brother. 'You are old enough to know better, Georgie. Paul is only a baby and some things scare him, even if they don't scare you.' Little did she know how I felt about the gruesome shadows and menacing movements of the cloth ceiling.

After the first few days of the monsoon the countryside changed dramatically from a brown, arid landscape to a panorama of rich green. Grass seemed to sprout on every barren rock and hillock. For some reason this reminded me of the time when my father made a bridge across the Ganges canal at Hardwar, and demonstrated its safety by sending my mother, Paul and me across it on the back of the five-ton elephant, Rani. The effect of the former and the strength of the bridge seemed equally miraculous.

No such excitements awaited us at Sholapur. My father inspected flood damage to bridges and railway lines in the district in the company of one or other of his resident engineers, and we remained at home with our mother, bored with indoor pursuits and sitting quietly looking at books. We began to be as eager for the monsoon to be over as we had been for it to begin.

The Monsoon is Over: The Brilliant Scene, Flowers and Flamboyants

At last, as September drew to a close, storms became less frequent and then, as if a switch had been turned off, the monsoon was over. Trees suddenly burst into leaf. The flamboyants which lined many of the roads in Sholapur came into dazzling colour. This was a wonderful time of year. The days were clear and pleasantly warm, and there was a freshness in the evenings which made going to bed a snuggling up enjoyment.

My mother planted English seeds — sweet peas, petunias, phlox, balsam and clarkias, which, by Christmas time were in full flower. Much of this was assisted by the abundance of manure from our own stables. The display of blooms could not have been bettered in any English garden.[6] Envious glances were cast by the other ladies of the station who did not have my mother's 'green fingers'.

Paul and I have both created lovely gardens in various parts of the world, and our sister has only recently retired from a most remunerative job as landscape gardener to some prosperous Arabs who have large grounds in the London region.

The Approach of Christmas

As Christmas approached social activities for the adults increased. On many evenings our mother would come to kiss us good night wearing a pretty dress, jewellery and sweet-smelling perfume. She and my father would be going out to a dinner party or to dance at the club. Sometimes they were hosting a dinner party in our own house.

---

6. It is interesting to discover from his memoir the example that had been set for him by his mother in India so long ago. (RT)

A Glimpse of the Dinner Party,
Ladies and Uniforms, Candles and Candelabra

We enjoyed it when they gave a dinner party. We could hear the carriages and cars arrive in our driveway, the voices raised in greetings. We glimpsed some of the ladies as they flitted past our open bedroom door on the way to my mother's room to make final adjustments to their toilettes; and often, when sounds from the dining room indicated that the guests were sitting down to dinner, we crept along the passage to the door of the sitting room and stared across to the dining room beyond. There men in dinner jackets or officers' uniforms sat round our dining table next to women in evening dresses, eating and talking in the flickering light of candles.[7]

In Sholapur our bungalow was lit by oil lamps, the candelabra being used only on special occasions.

Christmas was really close when we could see the decorations that were put up in the Sholapur Club. The club was used for adults, but we children knew it well, for we had to spend long hours amusing ourselves there whilst our parents were engaged in events from which we were excluded. There were swings and seesaws, but, for the most part, we ran about in the grounds playing tag or ball games with the other children. Our parents could be playing tennis, croquet or bridge.

At about six o'clock we were rounded up by our *ayah*s and taken home for our supper, whilst our parents stayed on for drinks with friends before coming home to dinner. When we passed the club windows as the lamps were being lit, we could see the Christmas tree sparkling with baubles and tinsel, and knew we had not long to wait for the children's Christmas

---

7. At such dinner parties in the early 1920s, virtually all the guests would have been Europeans. From 1919 onwards, however, with the introduction of the Montagu-Chelmsford Reforms, the situation changed and by the end of 1937, when my father left India, the guests at social occasions of all kinds included a great many Indians. (RT)

party. The tree, a large one reaching almost to the ceiling, was brought all the way from the distant Nilgiri Hills.

Children's Party at the Club
This party was arranged by lady club members, assisted by some of the young subalterns from the British contingent stationed at Sholapur.

Fathers showed little interest in arrangements for children's parties, so the younger and prettier wives often found themselves the objects of much attention from the young unmarried subalterns. The preparations were carried out in a light-hearted, somewhat flirtatious way, causing some of the elderly matrons to purse their lips. 'Old Mother Grundies', our mother called them. 'It's only harmless fun! And those young men seldom see a woman.'

I was puzzled about her remark, for there were lots of women in Sholapur, and some of the Eurasian ones were young and very pretty. Much later I realized that only European women — not Indians or Eurasians — were considered eligible.

However, whatever else they might have been doing whilst organizing the Christmas party, these mesdames and bachelors between them produced a wonderful afternoon's entertainment for us children.

We arrived neat and clean, wearing our white silk 'wedding suits'. All the other little boys wore similar suits, and the little girls were in party frocks. All had a fresh, scrubbed, well-combed look about them.

We gazed in quiet wonder at the array of presents stacked all round the Christmas tree, trying to divine the contents of the gaily wrapped parcels.

Father Christmas arrived smartly in what was supposed to be a sledge drawn by a couple of horses. He stomped into the club house with a lot of loud ho-ho-ing and began to distribute the packages stacked round the tree, calling out the names written upon them in a gruff voice. The pile of packages disappeared and, in no time, their place was taken by wrapping papers torn off and flung down by children eager to discover their gifts.

Sweating under his false beard and showing relief that his performance had come to a successful conclusion, Father Christmas stalked out the way he had come in.

Engines Red and Green

Paul and I began a tug-of-war over a painted wooden engine I thought was mine and he thought was his. Bigger and stronger, I soon had the engine away from him, and his mouth began to turn down at the corners. My mother, with the intuition possessed by all mothers, suddenly appeared. 'Give him back his engine,' she ordered.

'But it's *my* engine,' I said.

'It is not your engine,' my mother replied.

'That's your engine.'

She pointed to an identical wooden engine lying on the floor by my feet.

'No it isn't,' I insisted. 'mine's red.'

My mother stared at me. 'That one *is* red,' she said.

'No, Paul's got the red one,' I said.

'He's got the green one,' my mother said crossly, and then she looked hard at me, took Paul's engine from him, picked the other one from the floor, held both behind her back for a moment and then held them both out in front of her.

'Take the red one,' she said to me.

I reached out for the red one, and my mother gasped. I had taken the green one, and that is how it was discovered that I was colour-blind in red and green.

Other children, brothers and sisters, were arguing over each others' presents without valid excuses such as mine. Perhaps to prevent an outbreak of fighting before the party had really begun, a matronly lady banged the big brass gong that stood outside the dining room, and announced that tea awaited us in the marquee outside.

Out we rushed to get our fill of cakes, lemonade, jellies and trifles. It did not take long to gorge ourselves to bursting point, and we were soon out on the lawns eager for the best part of the day, the Children's Fair.

We took part in egg-and-spoon races, sack races, three-legged races and a tug of war. After these competitive sports came the delights of a coconut shy and a hoop-la stall.

The Aunt Sally

Finally, joy of joys, it was time for the Aunt Sally.

The Aunt Sally was like a bigger, better and real-life coconut shy. Aunt Sally had to be a very good sport, and it was usually one of the young subalterns who volunteered for the part. It involved wearing a woman's hat of an unfashionable variety resembling a felt pudding basin, and hiding inside a barrel, popping one's head up every now and then, to give children armed with tennis balls the opportunity of letting fly at one, with the object of scoring a direct hit on one's face which, preferably, should be adorned with a big grin. Since the distance between the Aunt Sally and the children, marked by a line, was considerable, there was not much danger to the former from the latter. But we flung our tennis balls at 'her' with intent to cause serious bodily harm. After a few goes of hammering Aunt Sally we were thoroughly excited. And then, at the climax of our excitement, the Punch and Judy Show was announced.

After the show it was time to go home. As we made our way reluctantly the club grounds, I noticed Aunt Sally talking to the pretty young wife of the manager of the cotton mills, and his expression suggested that he was really enjoying a rarely seen spectacle.

After the festivities of Christmas and the New Year, life settled down to a slower tempo.

Hot Weather Approaches

The pleasant weather lasted through January, but during February it was very hot. Thereafter it would get hotter and hotter. This was the time when it was thought advisable for women and children to go to a hill station.

From central India we used to go to Mussoorie, but that was a three-day journey from Sholapur, so my father decided that we would go to Kohnoor in the Nilgiri Hills (the blue hills), only a day and a night's journey away from Sholapur.

To Kohnoor in the Blue Hills

The days before our departure were hectic. Although Kohnoor was nearer than Mussoorie, there were no hotels or boarding houses, none of the conveniences or attractions of Mussoorie, and it possessed only one small store, which stocked basic essentials.

The nearest large centre was Bangalore, a day's journey away. My father had to rent a bungalow for us. We had to provide ourselves with all the impedimenta needed for running a household. Since my mother and we children would be remaining at Kohnoor for almost four months (the duration of the hot weather), the packing was formidable.

At last all was ready. My father's railway coach was crammed with luggage: trunks, wicker hampers full of clothing, bed linen, pots and pans and miscellaneous paraphernalia. Our *ayah*s, Rashid our assistant bearer and Ali our assistant cook were all with us.[8] Finally, we took with us our bulldogs,

8. During the Second World War, when I was in the Arakan–Burma frontier region, I was given two short spells of leave in Indian hill stations, to recuperate from jungle sores and general exhaustion. On both occasions my baggage consisted of only a kitbag and a very small suitcase purchased in Calcutta. I was beset by Indians of low castes who pressed me to engage them as bearers, assistant bearers, cooks, assistant cooks, gardeners, water-carriers, messengers and washermen. I stayed at hotels whose services were excellent, but my seeming independence was cruelly bewildering for people who were hardly aware of the war on their own frontiers. (RT)

Minka and Michael, and their baskets.

Ahmed and Yusuf, the young cook, were left behind to serve our father, who would only be spending a couple of weeks with us at Kohnoor.

I remember little of our stay at Kohnoor, except that Minka gave birth to half a dozen beautiful bulldog puppies whilst we were there; I still have a photograph of Paul and myself admiring them, whilst the proud mother lay to one side suckling them. I presume that the puppies travelled back to Sholapur with us. Our parents probably sold them or gave them away to friends. For some time Paul and I could hardly let the puppies out of our sight.

Kohnoor could not have been an unqualified success because our next hot weather was spent at Mussoorie, despite the travelling involved.

Five Already
Soon after our return to Sholapur I had my fifth birthday. I recall nothing special about that particular birthday, but I know from subsequent birthdays that on those days we children were allowed to choose whatever food we wanted for lunch and supper. At five years of age I had not yet developed a special fondness for anything, but I did love bananas and ice cream, which at that time were not often available. My mother had ice cream especially made for me. I remember very well, however, that after that birthday I was 'five'. Five had some special meaning for my parents. They spoke of it as 'being five already and still running wild', and decided that 'something must be done about it'.

Mrs Phillips, Spectacles and Garters
So one day I was taken to a nearby bungalow in which one of the resident engineers lived with his wife, and my mother introduced Mrs Phillips to me as 'your teacher'. My academic education was about to commence.

Mrs Phillips had been a teacher before her marriage. In a small summerhouse in her garden she was now running a little school. I was her second pupil, the first being a little girl who had also reached the miserable age of five, when freedom such as we had known it was lost, to return only after one of the birthdays of our sixties, when men are liberated from their bondage to employers.

Mrs Phillips tried to teach us the alphabet and how to count to ten on our fingers. Simple sums and the multiplication tables followed as we progressed.

Sitting still for long periods had never before been part of my lifestyle. Learning that A was for Apple, B for Bat, and that One and One are Two did not command my complete attention; and there was little to look at apart from the blackboard, the teacher's desk and the teacher. It was the last that I looked at most. She was a quite attractive woman, but she wore glasses. I had not previously noticed spectacles that were worn continuously. Grandpa Roche wore them when reading, but not for talking. Mrs Phillips's lenses caught the light at odd moments, winking back into my own eyes. This caused me to gaze steadfastly up into Mrs Phillips's face. She may have considered me a very attentive pupil.

It was not long before another sight caught my eye, teacher's legs. Unlike my mother, my teacher wore skirts that were relatively short for the period. Whenever she sat down at her desk it was possible to see up her skirt, to the region where her stockings ended in coloured garters above her knees, an expanse of white thighs disappearing into darkness. Once seen, this sight became compelling. I spent most of my time in that so-called classroom staring up my teacher's legs, fascinated by silk stockings, frilly garters and white thighs.

School, thank goodness, was restricted to mornings only, and at noon I could run home to join my younger brother who still enjoyed his freedom. When he asked why he could not go to school with me, he was told 'next year'. This made Paul happy, and it was not for me to disillusion him if he was actually looking forward to lessons with Georgie.

The Pretty Lady

One day on my way home from lessons I found that if I walked through the front garden next door to that of Mrs Phillips and out through the compound at the back of it I could shorten my journey considerably and come out almost immediately opposite our own bungalow.

On one occasion when I was about to take this route I saw a young woman in the garden. As I prudently removed my foot from the driveway, she looked in my direction and saw me. 'Were you coming here?' she asked. Because she was so pretty and smiled as she spoke, I felt that I need not deny my intention so I replied: 'Sometimes I take a shortcut through the garden. Our bungalow is on the other side.'

'Come on in then.' She smiled at me again. 'I shan't stop you.'

As I hurried through the garden I thought what a nice lady she was. As soon as I got home I asked my mother who lived next door to Mrs Phillips.

'John Roberts,' she replied.

John Roberts was the other resident engineer who worked with my father, but I had never heard any mention of a Mrs Roberts, and wondered aloud if Mr Roberts was married.

'No,' my mother replied. 'Why?'

'Well, there's an awfully nice lady in his garden and she didn't mind at all when she saw me taking a shortcut through it.'

'Oh!' My mother raised her eyebrows.

My mother did not answer my question, and I assumed that she could not have been very interested in the subject because she began at once to ask me what I had learnt at school that morning. On the same evening my father said that I should not trespass on other people's grounds. When I said that the lady in the garden had said she did not mind, my father simply said: 'But *I* mind you going there when you have not been invited.'

But She is Gone

The subject was not referred to again, and since I convinced my self that the lady's permission was as good as an invitation, I continued to cross the garden, but I never saw the nice lady again.

It would be some time yet before I became aware that Mr Roberts was one of those bachelors who 'seldom see a woman', an eligible white woman, that is, and had formed 'a relationship' with a very attractive Eurasian woman, and that such arrangements were frowned upon by white matrons, particularly those with spinster relations, who were most certainly white but whose other attractions were less conspicuous.

Mr Roberts must have been told promptly by my father that his mistress had been indiscreet enough to let herself be seen by a small white boy.

The memory of this incident came back to me many years later, after the independence of the sub-continent in 1947. During a visit to Lahore I was engaged on a project for a company and wanted the co-operation of the colonel of a regiment stationed there. The colonel was a British officer who had stayed on after partition. He was most helpful and we socialized frequently, my wife and I spending many enjoyable evenings with him and his Eurasian mistress, until the arrival of one of the directors of my company put an end to all friendly co-operation. One look at this very sophisticated Eurasian woman and the director promptly set about doing everything he could to seduce her himself.

But in 1920 in Sholapur it was expected that a gentleman should take pains to ensure that his mistress was not identified by white women and children. In 1921 the New Year was ushered in at the Sholapur Club with the song and dance common the world over, but Paul and I were too young to know anything of the revels after we were in bed and asleep.[9]

New Year's Day: Special Tiffin

New Year's Day was different. My parents invited friends for tiffin (lunch), and the party lasted all day, children arriving with their parents during the morning. By mid-afternoon all of them were as dishevelled as we were, after playing hide and seek all over the garden and the compound. Hiding in the compound was actually cheating, for visiting children could not make free of the servants' quarters when we were taken to their houses as we could in our own home. When in their houses we had to play games according to their rules.

January: Uncle Lawrence, Aunty Rie and Baby Cynthia

Whilst the ordinary routines of life returned in January, we were expecting visitors before the month was out. Uncle Lawrence and Aunty Rie (for whose wedding in London our own still serviceable silk suits had been purchased) were coming to stay, bringing their three-month-old daughter with them.

My uncle Lawrence had qualified as a doctor just before the outbreak of war in 1914, and he had immediately joined the Royal Army Medical Corps. His war service had been very distinguished, for he had been awarded both the Military Cross and the Croix de Guerre for gallantry in tending wounded and dying men on the battlefield under fire. After

9. During the eighteenth century and until after the opening of the short sea route to India via Alexandria and the Red Sea, British officers commonly had Indian or Eurasian mistresses, and there was no objection to it by either Indians or Europeans. The short sea route, however, brought great numbers of European women to India, many of them in search of British husbands. The racist attitudes described by George Roche originated in that epoch. (RT)

the war he was posted to a military hospital in England, where he married Rie, and they had not expected to be posted abroad for some time, but with promotion to the rank of captain came a posting to Rawalpindi, near the north-west frontier of India.

Just before their ship arrived at Bombay, their baby Cynthia had become ill, and Rie refused to travel all the way to Rawalpindi with a sick child. She knew that her brother-in-law had a comfortable bungalow, with servants, at Sholapur, much nearer to Bombay than Rawalpindi. My mother, too, would provide a shoulder to lean on, and she knew nobody else in India. They would have to stay with us until Cynthia had fully recovered.

The baby looked sickly and miserable, obviously in great pain, emitting shrill screams as she drew her stick like legs up to her chest. She had constant diarrhoea, her little yellow face wet with sweat. Uncle Lawrence diagnosed enteric fever. Aunty Rie and my mother hovered about the infant constantly, dripping glucose in boiled cooled water on to her lips, in the hope that some fluid would trickle into her mouth to prevent complete dehydration. Every now and then a tiny drop of chlorodyne was added to the mixture to dull the pain of the gastric spasms.

Years later I would treat myself and my own children in the same manner when gastric ailments troubled us in faraway places where no doctors trod.

Off to Rawalpindi

Cynthia gave Rie and Lawrence sleepless nights for a week and then began to recover. My uncle had cabled the reason for the delay in his journey to his commanding officer, but could postpone his departure for Rawalpindi no longer. He hoped that gentleman would be sympathetic, but knew that he could be in for a severe reprimand. Rie was reluctant to leave us, and they departed in a state of gloom and despondency, Rie muttering about the health hazards that would surely claim their lives in this primitive country to which they had been posted.

I was too young to appreciate the concern of mothers about the health of their infants in primitive conditions. Two wives and four children later I have got the message. As a child I thought how grumpy my uncle had become after only two years of married life.

Learning to Swim

Shortly after their departure for Rawalpindi, my father decided that Paul and I were old enough to be taught how to swim, and he had discovered the very place to give us lessons.

About five miles away there was a delightful and little-known spot. A tributary of the Bhima River flowed through a valley with a narrow flood plain on either side. Shady trees were dotted about and on one side the ground sloped upwards from the river and culminated in a semicircle of small hills overhanging the scene, resembling a park-like amphitheatre. Here one could walk along the banks of the river, which glinted and sparkled in the sunlight.

On the high ground beneath the hills were traces of the foundations of barracks that had housed a British cavalry regiment during the Maratha War of 1843. There was crumbling evidence of the stables. Another relic was a rackets court, with its high 'strike' wall and two wing walls tapering to the ground. The whole structure was falling to pieces, with weeds sprouting from the walls and the surface of the old court.

The Old Cantonment

Such derelict courts dating back to pre-Mutiny days could be seen all over India wherever a cantonment had been established. This one near Sholapur would have been played upon by regimental officers. Now the widening cracks and holes had become the haunts of numerous cobras, which bred there and could often be seen gliding down holes at one's approach.

The cantonment needed water, and a supply had been engineered by the construction of a furrow along which water gravitated from the upper reaches of the little river and flowed into a series of large sunken tanks made of bricks lined with old-fashioned lime mortar.

Water from the furrow also filled an ancient, dilapidated swimming pool surrounded by a wall and overshadowed by an enormous fig tree. Here officers would have cooled off after their exercise on the rackets court, or taken leisurely swims on hot afternoons, grateful for the shade provided by the tree.

The site for the cantonment had evidently been selected with care. So why had it been abandoned so many years ago in favour of the small, arid site which housed the present contingent? The most likely reason was the scourge of malaria. Although water was plentiful and the river scene idyllic during the day, the marshy fringes of the stream bred voracious mosquitoes which, together with a myriad of fire-flies, hummed as soon as darkness fell.

This theory was borne out by the crumbling monuments erected in the nearby military cemetery. For every stone over the grave of a soldier killed in action, there were two for those who had 'died of the fever'.[10]

My father had found that the swimming pool was empty because the water had leaked out through cracks in the masonry. He got some of our labourers to fill the cracks with fresh lime plaster, and the pool was again filled with water. Its cool depths awaited our hot, sticky bodies, for we had travelled in the wicker sidecar in the heat of the afternoon. We

10. Similar cemeteries, with sculpted marble monuments to the memory of young British soldiers, their wives and children, all of whom had died 'of the fever of the country', the cause of which was unknown, can be seen in many parts of the tropical world. There is a very moving example in St John's Church in Antigua, for long the capital of the Leeward Islands. (RT)

stripped quickly and stood beside our father for our first lesson.

We scrambled into the shallow end and found ourselves up to our necks in water. Standing over us, our father told us to lie on our backs and let the water hold us up. He explained that before we could learn to swim we had to learn how to float. Once that was mastered we could never drown. We were quite ready to obey him, never doubting that the water would in fact hold us up if he said it would.

We had gone through the motions of breast-stroke lying on cushions at home, and also at the pool side, lying on our towels, under the eagle eye of our father. We stood on either side of Papa and waited for him to tell us to get into the water. But, without a word, he just pushed us both into the pool. We came up gasping and flapping our arms about. We did not turn over on our backs, as instructed, or lie still, as in floating, but, swallowing mouthfuls of water, sneezed it down our noses, spluttered, gasped and blinked. Neither drowning nor floating we moved around in the water, probably in an atrocious display of dog-paddling. The achievement filled us with joy.

After that it did not take long for both of us to swim. It was learning to swim properly that took time.

On most afternoons we went to the site of the old cantonment for swimming lessons, and enjoyed ourselves very much. We explored the ruins of the stables and the rackets court, pretending to be cavalry officers at the time of the Mutiny. When we tired of this we could wander down to the river, play with a ball, chase each other and play 'I spy'. Whilst we played my father sometimes swam up and down the old pool enjoying his solitude, or sat in the shade of a tree and read a newspaper.

A Special Turtle
One day after our swimming lesson, we were passing the

water tanks on our way to play when Paul noticed a turtle sitting on the bottom of one of the tanks. The water was clear, and we could see that this particular turtle was very special because it had white spots on its back, quite unlike the plain brown backs of ordinary turtles, of which there were many.[11]

Paul immediately wanted to possess the turtle. He was passionately fond of living creatures, be they furry and cuddly, scaly and crawly or wriggly, and he implored my father to dive down 12 or more feet to the bottom of the tank and collect the turtle for him.

But Very Fierce

Anxious to examine this rare specimen himself, my father dived into the tank as quietly as possible, grabbed the turtle and brought it to the surface with a flourish. Paul was clasping his hands with glee as my father neared the side of the tank with his prize and held it out to him. Paul seized it with delight. By now the turtle was wide awake and no doubt furious at being so unceremoniously disturbed. It wiggled its flippers frantically in an attempt to escape, but little Paul held it tightly, peering intently at its lizard-like face. 'Nice turtle, pretty turtle,' he crooned with rapture. At that moment the turtle suddenly shot out its snout and gripped Paul's lip in its parrot-like beak, and there it hung, all three or four pounds of it, with no apparent intention of letting go. Paul's piercing screams brought my father, who had been drying himself nearby, to his side. My father had great difficulty in prising open the turtle's beak, but eventually managed it. The creature dropped to the ground and scuttled off back to the tank.

11. This was a carnivorous turtle, of which there are three main varieties, namely the loggerhead (*Caretta caretta*); the snapper (*Chelydra serpentina*) and the giant leathery turtle (*Sphargis coriacea*), which can reach almost eight feet in length and weigh as much as half a ton. The one described by the auther was a snapper. (RT)

Paul's lip was bleeding profusely from a nasty-looking gash. Mother bathed and applied iodine to it, which produced more screams from the child, but the treatment was effective and the lip healed well.

The episode temporarily cured Paul of his love of turtles. However, later on there will be another story about turtles. The next love of Paul's life was to be Ermintrude, a small female monkey, but before she appeared we went up to Mussoorie for another break from the hot weather.

ABOVE. The bungalow at Manmad in Nasik district, about 50 miles N.E. of the city. Very early in 1915. A corrugated iron structure typical of those allocated to junior officers of the G.I.P (Great Indian Peninslar Railway). Roberta in foreground before the birth of George. Photograph by Robert Roche.

RIGHT. Roberta in the garden of the bungalow at Manmad. Early 1915, before the birth of George. Photograph by Robert Roche.

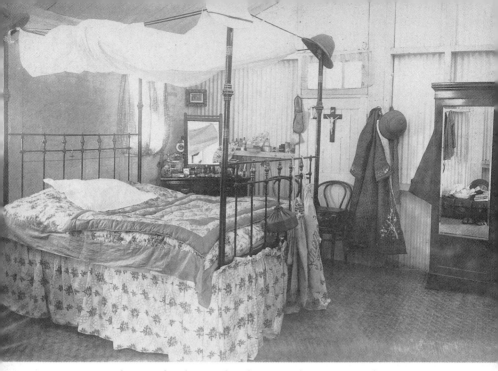

ABOVE. Bedroom of Robert and Roberta Roche at Manmad, circa 1915. George was born in this room. Photograph by Robert Roche. BELOW. The lounge at Sholapur circa 1920. The ornamental plates on the left were destroyed by the monkey Ermintrude (see p.55, 63-5). Note the elephant tusk carved with elephants graded in size, a relic of Robert Roche's East African war service.

ABOVE. The bungalow at Sholapur circa 1920. George and Paul in the background. The "Indian" motorcycle and wicker sidecar in the foreground. Various servants. Photograph by Robert Roche.

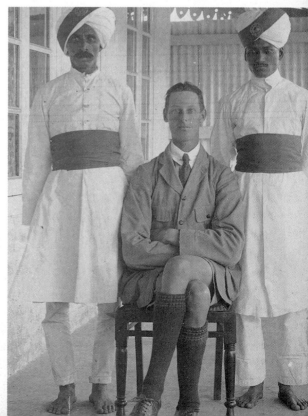

RIGHT. Robert Roche and two uniformed bearers. Early 1915. One of the bearers served Robert Roche throughout his career. Photograph by Roberta Roche.

ABOVE Captain George Roche (left), Royal Engineers, with Lieutenant Philip Morris of the Rifle Brigade, at the Southern extremity of the El Alamein Line, on 17 July, 1942, which was George's 27th birthday.

LEFT. Memorial to Roberta Roche, 1927. (See p. 127)

5
Mussoorie

Mussoorie was a bustling hill station. There were several hotels and boarding houses, many of them run by genteel widows of army officers. This saved all the bother of bringing household goods and most of the servants when one went to stay there.

My mother knew Mussoorie well because she had spent most of the years of the First World War there, when my father was away on the East African campaign.

She, left alone with a small child and expecting another, had stayed in one of the boarding houses.

Even before the Mutiny of 1857/8, the armies of the East India Company (namely those of Bengal, Bombay and Madras) used Mussoorie as one of the main hill stations to which the wives and families of British officers were sent for the hot weather. There was an excellent hospital and Paul was born there at the end of September 1916.

We had tried Kohnoor at my father's request. Now we were bound for Mussoorie at my mother's.

Doolies *and Baskets*
Going up to Mussoorie was always exciting from the moment we left the rail terminus at Dehra Dun. On the platform stood numerous *doolies*. These were chairs held between two poles

and carried on the shoulders of four men. Women were always taken up the winding path, rising to some 7000 feet above the plain, to the cool altitude of Mussoorie, sitting in those *doolies*. At the sight of my mother all the carriers surged expectantly forward, hoping for custom. Bigger children were put into a basket-like contraption. Inside was a seat for the child to sit on. Basket and child were hoisted on to a single carrier's back, and held in position by a strap around the forehead of the carrier. Bent almost double, he began the long haul up the steep ascent, the child quite unaware of how serious the situation could become if the man were to stand upright to stretch his shoulders.

This did not happen, but plenty of other harrowing things did. During such hauls frequent rests were needed. On one such rest the carrier to whose forehead my own basket was strapped, sat down upon a low wall and calmly smoked a *bidi* (a cigarette rolled from a single small leaf of tobacco), whilst the basket on his back in which I sat dangled over a precipice with a drop of 3000 feet between me and the ground.

The men would hire small wiry hill ponies at Dehra Dun and ride up to the hill station, the *syce* following on foot in order to ride the pony back down again after the *sahib* had reached his destination.

At the height of the hot weather the railway station at Dehra Dun was crowded with competitors for the carrier trade.[1]

---

1. Dehra Dun is still the rail terminus, but passengers for Mussoorie ascend the zig-zagging road either by car or in buses. In 1980 I travelled in an old bus packed to capacity with passengers, baggage and children. I was the sole European. It was a hot journey, the heat generated by the steaming, fuming engine.

The aspect of Mussoorie in modern India presents contrasts with its appearance in George's childhood, or when I stayed there on recuperative leave after a campaign in the Arakan in 1944. Many of the former hotels stand empty — white-painted wooden buildings standing prominently on the forested hillsides, forlorn relics of the past, dead flies lying upon their

As we climbed upwards the temperature dropped about five degrees for every 1000 feet of ascent, so that at Mussoorie the temperature was some 35 degrees below that in the plains. The climate there was very like that of England, but the sun always seemed to be shining. There were showers similar to those of April in England, leaving the hills glistening with small waterfalls and shiny rock faces. In winter snow would fall and Mussoorie would sometimes be cut off from the plains, but we only went there in the hot weather.

In such an equitable climate European fruit grew in abundance. Strawberries, raspberries, apples and pears were available. My mother once pointed out to me an Indian hawker walking with a tray of strawberries towards the market. As he went he methodically picked up each strawberry and gave it a good lick with his tongue, to make it nice and shiny, arranging it attractively on the tray, all dewy fresh. 'Never, ever,' said my mother, 'eat any fruit that has not been washed in *pinki-pani* [pink water].' The pinkness was produced by crystals of potassium permanganate dissolved in water. This was supposed to afford protection against the manifold germs and kinds of dirt assumed to smother all fruit and vegetables in India.

But I have been running ahead. My father on a pony, my mother in a *doolie*, Paul in his basket and I in mine journeyed

windowsills and floors. In those rooms, and upon deep tiled verandahs, we had danced through the nights with the girls of all the communities that had served in India's auxiliary wartime organizations. The hill station today is thronged in the hot weather with Indian families doing their own catering in self-contained apartments, as in most holiday resorts in Europe or America. The town also contains many private schools. In 1980 I stayed in a large building formerly owned by an Indian maharaja, now converted into a hotel, with very few guests and winding, dark passages, affording opportunities for bumping the head against invisible beams. (RT) up the steep winding track until at last, after about four hours, we reached Mussoorie.

Balu Gunge

We stayed in a well-run boarding house at a place called Balu Gunge (the bear's lair), tucked away in a wooded area about two miles from the town centre.[2]

The place was well named, for Himalayan bears still roamed the woods in those days, as did panthers, which often took domestic dogs and ate them.

My mother tended to over-dramatize the danger to us of confrontations with wild animals, filling us with alarm about what could happen to small boys. Paul and I often lay in our beds imagining animals prowling round the boarding house.

One morning I awoke before dawn to the sound of noises in the garden. I got out of bed, crept to the window and looked out. My heart nearly stopped. On the front lawn a large bear was trying to shake the fruit from a medlar tree, which normally gave shade to residents taking tea beneath its branches.

Not far from Balu Gunge was a derelict building, which had been an officers' mess at the time of the Mutiny. The name 'Skinner's Horse' was still etched on the old brick gateposts. It had been the hot-weather retreat for the famous cavalry regiment raised by Captain Skinner. They roamed far and wide, striking terror into the hearts of the mutineers and earning a reputation for utter fearlessness.

The Old Brewery

Balu Gunge had plenty to interest children. There was the ruin of an old brewery. We children were told never to go inside because the floor-boards of the various galleries were so rotten that they could give way beneath our feet, causing falls

2. I found the boarding house full of Indian guests in 1980. (RT)

of several feet to certain injury. We obeyed this instruction at first, but later could not resist the temptation to explore the place. One day my father caught us there and gave us both a thrashing.

Today it seems so strange, but when I was a child it was quite usual for a parent to beat a child almost to death in the interests of saving its life.

Pneumonia and 'Crisis'

It was not only children who were casual about their safety. Just nearby there was a very old swimming pool, fed by a mountain stream, which cascaded down a sluice into icy cold water. It was exciting to climb to the top of the sluice and to slide down the algae-slippery sluice into the pool. This was supervised by my father, himself a good swimmer, to make sure we did not drown. However, on one occasion Paul was allowed to splash about in the near freezing water perhaps for too long, for he caught pneumonia. He was rushed to the hospital in which he had been born.

I recall the great anxiety of my parents as they waited for 'the crisis', and their great happiness when told that Paul was 'over the crisis'. I went with my mother to collect him. He looked very wan, but was in fact well again. For a long time afterwards he had special treatment, much rest and plenty of nourishing food. It seemed to me that he had to have a lot of his own way. At last he was allowed to run wild with me again, but none of us, including my father, was permitted to slide down the sluice into the pool again that season.

A Grim Spectacle

We enjoyed going for walks with our mother. We would run ahead of her as she strolled leisurely behind us along the pathways winding round the hillsides. On one such outing we spotted a small brick structure some distance below us, and ran down to investigate. It was a small hut with a rickety-looking door on broken hinges. We pushed it open and stood utterly aghast. There was a complete human skeleton with tattered clothing clinging to the bones. We stood stock still and stared. Then, speechless and trembling, we ran back, almost sobbing, to our mother. Convinced by our bloodless faces, she accompanied us back down the hill to see for herself.

Her reaction was similar to our own except that she closed her eyes and backed out of the hut, holding both of us tightly by the hand.

Whilst we had been running up and down the hillside we had been just aware of a tall, dark Pathan leaning on the parapet wall along the pathway above us. As we returned with our mother from the hut we noticed him watching us intently, but as soon as we got near to him he moved off rapidly.

Pathans had a reputation for ruthless cruelty in the North-West Frontier region, and he certainly looked forbidding. The local Pathans, however, were mostly traders, selling their usual carpets to womenfolk at the hill station.

The Murderer!

As soon as we got back to the boarding house our mother sent one of the servants to the police station with a note about the skeleton. Shortly afterwards, an inspector called to thank my mother for the information, and he questioned us about the exact location of the hut. Still later my mother heard that about 18 months earlier a man had disappeared from a nearby village after a quarrel with a Pathan over a woman, and that the Pathan had never been seen again.

Paul and I were convinced that the murderer was the Pathan we had seen staring at us from the parapet. It seems more likely that anyone who had committed the crime would have left the neighbourhood altogether. However, we feared that we could have been scooped up by the huge Pathan and flung over the parapet to our deaths on the rocks below. Back at

Sholapur we held our friends spellbound with our stories of the MURDERER, and the mother of the small girl Alice, who had joined the class by then, told us to stop harping on about murders and skeletons, for she, Alice, was having nightmares about them.

The Story of Ermintrude

One day an Indian urchin came to our bungalow holding a young female monkey by a piece of rope round her neck. The unfortunate creature could not long have been parted from its mother and was pathetically skinny. Paul felt that at last his wish to own a monkey might be granted. And sure enough, after a little pleading, my mother gave the Indian child a few coins and the monkey changed hands. The monkey clung to Paul as though she had recognized her saviour.

Never was a monkey more cosseted than this stringy bundle of fur. A box with straw was found for her. Wire netting covered the box. The monkey was given a daily ration of diluted milk, which she sucked from the teat of an old baby's bottle. As she grew bigger, she progressed to a few ground-nuts and bananas. Eventually she was released from the box and allowed the run of the house, only returning to the box at night.

Most of the day she wandered about the garden, that is, when Paul let her out of his clutches, for he loved her dearly and a strong bond seemed to have been formed between them. For some reason the monkey was given the name of Ermintrude, and when she heard her name called she would come running in the hopes of being rewarded for her cleverness with a few nuts or a banana.

She became completely tame and seemed proud of the little leather collar my mother had fastened round her neck. She often perched on one or other of our shoulders and made chirping sounds of delight. Visiting friends were envious of our little playmate, and indeed Ermintrude gave us a lot of pleasure and continued to do so for some months. Then, without any warning, she suffered a personality change and went berserk.

One morning, when Paul went as usual to remove the wire netting covering her box, she leapt up and bit him. He shrieked, more in amazement than pain. I ran to see what was the matter and Ermintrude promptly leapt at and bit me too. My mother arrived on the scene followed by my father, and Ermintrude favoured each of them with a bite. My father made a grab at her, but she was too quick for him. She leapt nimbly up to the top shelf of the dresser in the dining room and began flinging the very fine bone-china dinner set down on the flagstones below.

My mother was very proud of the dining plates which Ermintrude was dashing to pieces, and screamed at the monkey to stop. But Ermintrude threw every plate to the floor and demolished the lot. My parents' fury was fearful to see. My father and all the servants set about trying to catch Ermintrude and, after a furious chase, my father caught her and held on to her in spite of all her bites and scratches. A rope was tied to her collar and she was led out of the house to the bottom of the garden.

Paul and I did not witness the execution, but a loud bang from my father's 12-bore signalled that Ermintrude had met her end.[3]

3. Within a few years of George Roche's monkey story, I was a student at the University of London, and fell in love with an American fellow student. I described my experience to my father in a letter to him in India, where he was Chief Justice of Bihar and Orissa at the High Court of Patna. In a reply he issued a warning: 'To give a young man a virgin to woo and win is like giving a monkey a valuable china tea set for his meals.' I heeded the warning, but my student love was later killed in a car crash in the United States. (RT)

No great sorrow was felt by any of us at her departure. Our mother was extremely upset about her dinner service, which had been given to her by her own mother and was regarded as a family heirloom to be passed on to the next generation. The plates were now in fragments all over the dining room floor. She regarded them sorrowfully, for it was clear that they could never be made whole again.

My father was bitten and scratched at a time when he should have been working on some difficult plans, which he had brought home to deal with in peace in his study, instead of at the office. Paul and I were nursing our bites, which stung after the plentiful applications of iodine our mother insisted on giving us. We worried lest the bites would go septic, for we had overheard the parents of one of our friends gossiping about the folly of our parents in allowing a monkey to run about the house. Everyone knew they were treacherous creatures whose bites could be very nasty.

However, next morning we missed running to let Ermintrude out of her box. Paul was sad and wondered, 'Why did she do it?' So did I.

Sylvia. What is She?

Some time in 1921, shortly after the demise of Ermintrude, another female creature was to enter our lives. She was Sylvia Valery, the sister we had forgotten about in England, who had now been pronounced perfectly fit and able to travel to India to rejoin her family.

Our grandmother Roche had been asked by our father to engage a nursemaid to look after Sylvia on the voyage and thereafter to act as a governess to all three of us children. They were already on the ship bound for Bombay. We learnt about all this from the excerpts of a letter from our grandparents that had been read out to us.

Our Roche grandparents had been heartbroken at parting with the little girl they had looked after for almost three years, especially when my parents had only a short time to wait before their next home leave was due. This, however, had been quite deliberate. It was felt that Sylvia Valery should be exposed to the Indian climate gradually, joining us during the cold weather and returning with us to England when we went on leave.

Our grandparents' descriptions of Sylvia were so glowing that we regarded her as some juvenile saint or little angel, and we wondered how we could compete with such a paragon.

The nursemaid would be bringing Sylvia to Sholapur on the train any day. Paul and I waited with some trepidation. What effect would she have upon us boys, who had always been so close? How would she fit in with our games, which had never been designed to include girls?

The mention of a nursemaid who would metamorphose into a governess filled us with foreboding. Would it mean a further curtailment of our freedom? And would lessons now be conducted at all hours of the day? The immediate prospects looked gloomy, but we need not have worried.

The nursemaid was young, dark-haired, dark-eyed and very attractive, so much so that, before the ship docked at Bombay, she had become engaged to an officer who was returning to India to rejoin his regiment. We were not aware of this when she arrived at Sholapur station. Sylvia held her hand and did not seem keen to relinquish it to take my mother's. My father hugged the child and smiled at the nursemaid. My mother frowned slightly and indicated that we should move off the platform and make our way home.

Paul and I had driven to the station in the 'Indian' with our father and my mother had come in her pony trap, the idea being that Sylvia and her nursemaid would travel back to the bungalow in the trap with our mother. The damsel's luggage would be put on a *tonga*, which should follow our retinue.

As yet Sylvia had said no more than 'hallo' to anybody. But as soon as she saw Paul and me getting into the sidecar, she shouted, 'Me!' very loudly, ran after us and climbed in with us. There was no room for her, but she sat down on top of both of us and would not budge.

'She'll fall out, Rob,' our mother said. 'You can't ride with her sitting up like that.' My father lifted Sylvia up and she let out a scream. Paul and I looked at each other.

My mother and the nursemaid were sitting in the trap. My father deposited Sylvia on the nursemaid's lap, and she had to hold the wriggling and kicking child very tightly to prevent her flinging herself out of the trap. My mother cracked the whip and they trotted off. My father started up the motorbike. Paul and I were still looking at each other, but now we were grinning.

That evening Sylvia and the nursemaid joined Paul and me for supper. To introduce Sylvia to Indian-style food, we were given a simple dish of rice with lightly curried lentils (*dahl baat*), which Paul and I always enjoyed very much.

Sylvia had never been given any Indian food in England, our grandmother much preferring traditional English meals. She sampled one or two mouthfuls with obvious distaste. It was clear, too, that she was very tired; her eyelids were drooping. Her nurse excused her, gathered her up in her arms and carried her off to bed.

Paul and I finished our supper and went to the sitting room to say goodnight to our parents and to receive the usual hugs. In the bedroom Lela and Mina were waiting to get us ready for bed. As they undressed us they chatted excitedly in their own Maharashtra language, which Paul and I understood well. They were wondering how the little *memsahib* was going to settle down. We were wondering too, but did not have long to wait to find out.

Next morning Paul and I joined our parents at the breakfast table as usual, but now Sylvia and her nurse were at the table too. I can see the scene now as I write: the early-morning sunlight illuminating the table and the persons sitting round it — a tableau. Ahmed began serving breakfast from the sideboard: scrambled eggs on toast for the adults and boiled eggs with fingers of buttered toast for us children, another favourite dish, which our mother must have thought would appeal to Sylvia too.

Tibby Doesn't Like

Paul and I started topping our eggs, whilst the nursemaid topped Sylvia's for her. We dipped our fingers of toast into our eggs, eating with relish. The nursemaid dipped a finger into Sylvia's egg and conveyed it towards her mouth. Her reaction was astonishing. With a sudden movement of her small arm she swept all her buttered toast to the floor, which was strewn with broken china, egg and a mess of buttered toast. 'Tibby doesn't like,' she said emphatically.

Paul and I gaped at each other, expecting any minute that some dreadful retribution would descend upon our sister. We knew that if we had dared to behave as she had done our bottoms would have been sore for a week. Our parents, however, were so taken by surprise that they were speechless. Then, to our astonishment, my father uttered a mild rebuke:

'You must never do anything like that ever again, young lady.'

Sylvia glared mutinously at him.

'Tibby doesn't like,' she repeated doggedly.

Our grandparents had given her the pet name of 'Tibby', which she much preferred to her real name.

'Tibby will have to do as she is told,' our father said grimly, and Paul and I nodded sagely to each other in complete agreement with his dictum. *We* had to do as we were told. So why not Sylvia? Breakfast proceeded in silence whilst Ahmed quickly cleared up the mess, his face impassive as he bent about his task.

Finishing his breakfast, my father stood up, kissed my mother, said goodbye to us children and strode out of the

68

room to go to his office. Sylvia slid down out of her chair and made to follow him.

'Stay where you are!' my mother said sharply. 'You cannot leave the table until you have asked permission and been given it.'

Sylvia stared at her, but made no move to get back on to her chair.

Defiance was something our mother would never tolerate.

'Go to your room, Sylvia,' my mother said quietly, but Sylvia did not budge. My mother stood up, took Sylvia by the arm and propelled her out of the room. Anticipating fire-works, Paul and I scurried along to our bedroom to be nearer the scene of action. We strained our ears to hear what was being said, but our mother spoke softly, as she always did when she was most angry, and we could hear little.

My mother led Sylvia into her bedroom, deposited her inside, went out again and locked the door behind her. She went into her own bedroom and summoned the nursemaid to her. The nursemaid felt no need to talk in whispers. 'She's a very difficult child and you'll have your work cut out trying to teach her to be as obedient as your little boys,' she shouted.

Paul and I beamed at each other. Instead of Sylvia being held up to us as a model, it was we who were now being held up.

Rob! She's Gone!

More drama followed the next morning. Neither Sylvia nor her nurse appeared for breakfast. My mother marched to the bedroom they shared, knocked and went in. The room was empty. Back in the breakfast room, waving a piece of paper in her hand, she shouted to my father, 'Rob! She's *gone*!'

'What!' my father paled. Paul and I sat bolt upright with excitement. However, behind my mother trailed a very sleepy Sylvia still wearing her nightdress. It was not she who had gone, but the nursemaid. She had left a note to explain that she was off to be married to an officer she had met on the ship.

'Miss ... has gone,' my mother said. 'She's getting married.' She placed the piece of paper in front of my father.

'Might have known a pretty girl like that would get off on a ship full of army personnel,' he said. 'I'm surprised Mama engaged such a pretty girl to look after Sylvia.'

'No wonder the child is so naughty,' my mother said. 'I suppose that flighty girl was too busy flirting to pay any attention to her.'

I cannot remember the nursemaid's name but I do remember being glad she had turned out to be flighty enough to get off with an officer instead of becoming a governess for us.

None of us noticed that Ahmed carried Sylvia's breakfast away uneaten, but thereafter she seemed to have no appetite. In those days adults insisted that everything on a child's plate must be eaten. Day after day Sylvia would sit from lunch time to tea time with a plate of congealed, fatty meat and vegetables before her, and the same mass was presented to her at supper time. But she would not eat and I have never understood how she survived the lack of food and the numerous smackings meted out to her. Parents then were more feared than God himself. Anyway, we rejoiced in the continued nonemergence of a governess.

Today I can imagine that being uprooted from the home of our grandparents, where she had been the light of their elderly lives, and set down in a completely strange environment among people who were her kin but, for all she knew, might have been total strangers, must have been a very disturbing experience for a child of three. Seventy years ago sympathetic handling of such reactions was rare indeed. Sylvia was punished for what seemed to Paul and me to be downright rebellion. We had little sympathy for her and thought her foolhardy not to conform to the rules, as we had learned to do.

Up to Mischief

At about this time Paul and I became increasingly mischievous. I cannot explain this. It could have been a symptom of our age, or perhaps Sylvia's behaviour had influenced us. In particular we wanted to find out how the big 'Indian' motorcycle worked, despite stern orders from our father to keep away from it.

The 'Indian'

He had built a concrete ramp for the machine at the edge of the verandah so that the motorcycle could be driven right up to the shelter it provided, and there it stood idle almost every day when my father was working.

At first Paul and I were content to admire the machine, gazing at it and touching it reverently. But it was not long before we were climbing on to it and fighting for possession of the saddle, the weaker of us being relegated to the wicker-work sidecar in the role of a passenger. At first we thoroughly enjoyed the imaginary trips we made and the noises we uttered when voicing the sounds of the engine revving up, speeding and stopping. But soon I, for one, wanted to do more than pretend to drive the bike.

When sitting in the sidecar I had watched my father very closely when he started the engine and as he drove along, accelerating, slowing and stopping, and felt sure that I could copy his actions accurately enough to drive the bike myself.

My father was unlikely to give me an opportunity, so the only chance I had of achieving my ambition was to find an occasion when both parents and all the servants would be unlikely to notice what I was up to.

Eventually I thought the time had come. One day my parents gave a large curry lunch party to the general manager of the railway and his wife. Many guests arrived and our parents and the servants had been kept very busy entertaining and waiting upon them. When the last guest had gone in the heat of the afternoon and my parents went to their belated siesta, and the servants, after clearing up, had retired to the compound, where they also had their siesta, the opportunity had at last arrived.

Paul was almost asleep on his bed, but I roused him into activity. We crept along the verandah to the motorcycle. Paul was worried lest I might not be able to drive it, but I was fully confident that I knew exactly what to do.

Whenever he parked the machine my father would put it into gear, to prevent the wheels from moving. So my first job was to free them, which I managed to do quickly. We edged the vehicle close to the ramp, gave it an almighty heave and watched it roll down the ramp.

It came to rest in the driveway, just as I had wanted, for I intended to drive round the drive a couple of times before taking it out on the road.

Paul clambered into the sidecar and I began the serious business of starting the engine. I pulled and pushed everything I had seen my father pull and push before he kicked the starter into life. The starter posed a problem because it needed some weight to activate the lever, and I was not very heavy. But undaunted, I climbed onto the saddle and jumped down on the starter with both feet.

Wallopings for Two

The effect was terrifying. With a roar the big twin cylinders burst into life. Something I had pulled or pushed had opened the throttle wide. Desperately I struggled to pull or push something that would cut down the noise. But the uproar had awakened my father, who shot out of his bedroom and, in what appeared to me to be a single movement, turned off the engine and grabbed me, up-ended, for a tremendous walloping. 'Idiot boy!' he shouted. 'Do you want to kill yourself?'

Paul, meanwhile, had got out of the sidecar and was making a beeline for the bedroom, but there was no escape for him.

72

My father pounced on him and walloped him too, but not as hard as he had walloped me, for he began to protest that 'Georgie made me help him.'

'Got a mind of your own, haven't you, boy?' my father asked angrily, well aware that Humbi always wanted to do whatever I did. But I was the eldest and had endangered not only my own life, but Paul's as well, so deserved a harder lesson.

Daniel the Docile

Shortly after the motorcycle affair a new dog came to live with us, a liver-coloured spaniel called Daniel. His owners, friends of my father, were retiring to England and would have been obliged to have him put to sleep but for my mother's willingness to add him to our family of dogs.

He was quite a nice-looking animal and, like all spaniels, very affectionate, but having been the only pet of an elderly couple he lacked the aggressive spirit of our own dogs. They, Minka, Michael, Lucy and Topsy, subjected him to constant bullying, and he fled from all of them, even though Lucy and Topsy were much smaller than he was.

When my mother saw that our dogs were giving Daniel a hard time, she decided that he should be put under my care and protection, and she pronounced him to be Georgie's very own dog.

I had always wanted a dog of my own, but the animal I had in mind would have combined the dimensions of a young lion with the fighting spirit of our fox terrier Lucy. In the godown where the food for our horses was stored, I had seen Lucy kill six or seven rats in a few moments, catching them by the backs of their necks and breaking their backs with a smart flick.

However I decided that I could probably train Daniel to become the kind of dog I wanted, despite his timid and lethargic temperament.

On most evenings Paul and I would walk to the club, getting there in time to play about in the grounds for a while before walking home with our parents. I decided to begin Daniel's training programme by taking him on these walks and throwing sticks for him to fetch. Alas, he was not interested. His previous owners had never introduced him to the joys of doggy exercise and he was now too old to appreciate them. He followed me along docilely and it was not till half a century later, when I saw Barbara Woodhouse on TV that I realized that Daniel had got 'walking to heel' off pat, and had been trained to be a well-behaved and obedient dog.

The Bandicoot

At the club was a large sunken circular children's paddling pool. It was quite dry because the rainwater had soaked away through the large cracks that had developed in it. One evening we were surprised to see a large bandicoot (a large species of rat common in India) sitting disconsolately in a corner of it. It had evidently fallen in and was unable to get out by scaling the wall.

Here was a chance for Daniel to show his mettle.

'Here boy,' I hissed at Daniel and pointed at the bandicoot at the bottom of the empty pool.

Daniel showed not the slightest interest, and, since I had stopped walking, he too stopped and sat down on the edge of the pool.

This was too much for me. I seized him and pushed him into the pool with orders to 'Get him!', fully expecting that he would despatch the very large rodent as easily as Lucy dealt with rats in the godown. However, as soon as the bandicoot spotted the intruder it charged at it, and Daniel was chased yelping round and round the enclosure by the irate bandicoot. And the creature was gaining steadily. Daniel was no Lucy, and the next time he came round on his circuit I grabbed him and hoisted him to safety.

Whilst disappointed by Daniel's performance, I was alarmed by that of the bandicoot, which reminded me of the horrific experience of waking up on board the *Dufferin* to a nose-to-nose confrontation with a large rat sitting on my chest. Fury might prompt the bandicoot to jump out of the pool to attack me! I picked up several stones and hurled them at the animal. One of them must have struck it, for it fell and was quite still. I threw a few more to make sure and said to my younger brother: 'It won't do any harm now.'

Rudolf the Temperamental

If Daniel lacked all aggression, my horse Rudolf was showing more and more of it. Though becoming taller and stronger, I could hardly deal with him. I could not prevent him suddenly bolting home at full gallop during an evening ride, with me clinging on for dear life.

My mother became alarmed and I overheard my parents discussing whether it was advisable for such a strong and wilful horse to be ridden by a small boy. This made me more determined to master Rudolf. That was easier said than done.

I remember how he was acquired. There was a notice board in the club upon which people who were going on leave put up notices describing the articles and animals they wanted to sell. One such notice caught my mother's eye: 'Young horse, chestnut, about 14 hands, suitable as child's pony. Loves children.'

Rudolf was purchased and joined our other two horses in the stables. It would be hard to imagine a more unsuitable horse for children. He had a mouth like iron and no amount of tugging on an ordinary bit could deflect him from any direction he chose to follow. He was soon put on a curb, but that did little to restrain him. He would at first put on an air of demure docility, so that one was tempted to approach and pat him. Then he would roll his eyes, showing the whites, bring his rear round and kick out with both hind legs. As already mentioned, he once landed a hefty kick on my chest, sending me sprawling and leaving me with a bruise the shape of a horseshoe. He could bite, too. As one prepared to mount by putting one's left foot into the stirrup, he would swing round and give one a hard nip on the bottom.

My mother used to say that Rudolf had probably been maltreated as a colt, and was trying to get his own back. She was soft-hearted towards all animals and was especially fond of horses. My father never trusted them, perhaps because he had been knocked down in Brompton Square by a runaway horse and cab when he was a boy. They argued about the comparative merits of horses and engines. She was accustomed to driving a horse and trap, but was ill at ease in a car, complaining that my father drove too fast.

Going 'On Line'

My father often had to travel on the rail network to inspect, direct or oversee work throughout the Deccan.

Touring the lines on duty was called 'going on line', and we children loved being with our father on such occasions. It was like a holiday for us because all lessons were dispensed with and we were transported for miles through the countryside in the comfort of his special coach.

Shooting 'For the Pot'

My father once had to design and build a new bridge to replace one damaged during the previous monsoon.[4] The old bridge, spanning a small river, had broken down when the flood water descended upon it after very heavy rain. The new

---

4. In many parts of the tropical world, especially in Africa and India, the rainy seasons are devoted to agriculture. In the dry weather, for many weeks after the harvest, the soil becomes too desiccated and hard for tillage, and the people confine themselves largely to tasks such as repairing the roofs of huts, or making new walls. Travel at that time is delightful. (RT)

bridge had been built alongside it, and now the railway line must be diverted to pass over it, an operation expected to take about ten days. My father brought the whole family because the district was full of game, such as black buck, partridges and peafowl. In the evenings he would shoot game 'for the pot'. In those days shooting 'for the pot' was the accepted way of feeding oneself on tour in many branches of government, especially in the administrative and magisterial services, veterinary and forestry services, and, in this case, engineering. The officer concerned was expected to shoot the food required by his entourage of servants and, on this occasion, all the railworkers too.[5]

To Washimbi

When at last the day of our departure from Sholapur arrived our father told us that we would be going to a place called Washimbi, some distance away.

Our coach was crammed with a clobber of provisions (including big pots and pans, and clothing) and all the dogs were on the platform too — Minka and Michael the bulldogs, Lucy the fox terrier, Topsy of no known breed, and Daniel the docile. All the dogs (except Daniel) were rushing around, barking with excitement.

Our coach had been linked to a fast goods train and as soon as we were all aboard it pulled away from the platform and roared off towards Washimbi. We rushed through green, well-

5. Perhaps one of the most dramatic accounts of 'shooting for the pot' is that of Captain F. D. Lugard (later Lord Lugard) in the second volume (1893) of his great narrative *The Rise of our East African Empire*. He raised a ragged army of about 300 miscellaneous Arab and African volunteers in Mombasa and marched at their head all the way to Lake Victoria in Uganda, to put a stop to a devastating civil war at the request of the Kabaka of Buganda. Lugard personally shot all the game required for his little force, and accomplished his mission. Uganda did not become a British protectorate, however, till 1894. (RT)

watered countryside alongside 'the jungle', that exciting, dark entanglement, which we were forbidden to enter alone or on foot. It fascinated us. It was known that a pair of leopards lived in it, and men working on the lines described the remains of animals that had been killed. It was thought that tigers also lived there, and we shivered with excitement at the thought of them, hoping that we might see them from the safety of our fast-moving coach.

We arrived at Washimbi in the evening. The little station was a very pretty place, for the stationmaster had created a lovely garden round it. Our coach was shunted into a quiet siding and we settled down to spend the next ten days there.

The Inspection Trolley

'On line' Paul and I greatly enjoyed the opportunity of riding on the special 'inspection trolleys' used by railway staff for checking that the rails were in good order.

'Lorris Wallahs'

These trolleys were moved solely by manpower. A team of six men in red shirts and shorts, with the GIP sign on their top pockets, did the job. They were known as *lorris wallahs* and worked in relays. Two of them ran along the rails balancing themselves with great dexterity, their bare feet slapping on the steel, hot beneath the sun, pushing the trolley in front of them. The other four sat on the back of the trolley behind the bench seat. When the two pushers had done their stint they leapt up on the trolley and two of the others jumped down to take their places on the rails. The speed of the trolley did not exceed four or five miles per hour, but all the *lorris wallahs* would hop on the trolley and let it coast down any slope. Sometimes it rolled very fast indeed. There was a brake lever sticking up beside the bench seat, which enabled the inspectors on the seat to control the speed, but the trolley could never go too fast for Paul and me.

Paul and I loved to get on one of these trolleys with our father. We had been warned never to get on one without him, for only in the care of an experienced trolley *wallah*[6] like himself would we be safe. In the early evenings, when my father had finished work, he would take us on the trolley up or down the single-line track from Washimbi, in search of a likely spot for interesting game to observe, or common wild-life to shoot for the pot.

I, too, once used to shoot for the pot what I considered to be common wildlife, but, as I write this, I shudder to recall how cheerfully I had killed these unfortunate creatures, even if I did so to provide myself and my men with food in wartime.

I stopped shooting 30 years ago and did so abruptly. I was on a duck shoot on the Zambezi, and though my party was shooting for the pot, I realized that the paraffin refrigerators in our quarters would enable us to keep a lot of birds on ice, and that the 'bag' was already enormous. The sight of the large pile of dead birds we had shot on the wing suddenly filled me with remorse, and I have never shot anything since then. In fact from then on I became an ardent hunter of poachers and caught quite a few of them. But that was long, long after our adventures on the trolley with our father.

One evening the whole family had been out with Papa on the trolley. Perhaps for that reason we had not noticed that we were returning to Washimbi somewhat later than usual.

6. A common expression meaning 'fellow' or 'fella', usually a representative of some vocation. A *'boxwallah'* meant a trader, the word being associated with tradesmen who knocked on doors and requested permission to display the contents of a box carried on the head or on the back of a bicycle. British officials and army personnnel often derided the entire British commercial communities of Calcutta and Bombay as a lot of *boxwallahs*. After independence in 1947, however, it was the British *boxwallahs* who survived in India, together with their counterparts in Africa, Sri Lanka, Malaya and other parts of Britain's former tropical empire. (RT)

Before all expeditions with the trolley, my father checked with the stationmaster to see that the line was clear, and for how long it would remain so. 'Clear' meant that no trains were expected on the single-line track during a certain period.

Wrath of the Iron God

On this evening we children were half asleep; Sylvia was on my father's lap, Paul on my mother's and I was leaning against her. It was getting quite dark and my eyelids were drooping as we rounded a steep bend on an embankment. Then suddenly I awoke to the most fearful sight I had ever seen: an engine under full steam was bearing down upon us, steam hissing from its sides, pulling a goods train, sparks leaping like fireworks from its funnel. The noise was deafening and the track trembled beneath us. Many times in the Second World War I thought my end had come, but never with such certainty as on that night a mile or two from Washimbi.

Presence of Mind

Only about 100 yards separated us from that thundering train. Panic ensued. Mother and children screamed. My father, as always, kept his head. He yanked the brake lever and our wheels squealed to a halt.

In a flash he hurled my mother, sister and brother off the trolley to roll down the embankment. He threw his gun after us and, with supernatural authority commanded the terrified *lorris wallahs* to help him lift the trolley off the rails and threw it, too, down the slope. Sudden adrenalin worked, and the huge engine and trucks raced over the spot occupied by ourselves only seconds before.

It was dark then, and I wonder if the engine driver even suspected the tragedy that had been averted.

Terror had enabled me to hurtle down the embankment. I climbed back up again, however, just in time to see the twinkling rear lamp of the train's guard's van disappearing in the distance.

My father was already directing the *lorris wallahs* to help him right the trolley and put it back on the tracks. They were feverishly searching for the birds my father had shot, for he paid them for their 'overtime' with an equal share of the bag and they did not want any of that evening's bag to be lost.

Back on board the trolley, we children huddled against our mother, who was too shaken even to ask my father why a goods train had been hurtling along the track at a time when the line had been pronounced 'clear'.

That night I dreamt of a great dragon shrivelling me with his fiery breath, and awoke shivering. Then I remembered that we had escaped the wrath of the Iron God, and lay still.

However, the iron master was not to be deprived of his sacrifice altogether. We were all on the station at Washimbi waiting for our coach to be linked to the fast goods train bound for Sholapur. Minka and Michael, the bulldogs, were lying at our feet when suddenly a mongrel dog ran past them, jumped on to the rail and streaked under the wheels of our goods train. Minka and Michael dashed after the mongrel just as the engine pulling the train made a sudden leap forward. Both dogs were sliced in half without a yelp from either.

The whole family was shocked and we children wailed in anguish at the loss of these beautiful and loveable creatures.

Their remains were buried under a tree and we returned to Sholapur with memories of how they used to let us try to ride on their backs, run and fetch balls for us and submit to rough, playful handling from us with never an unpleasant growl.

Back at home our parents began to prepare for leave in England, and to talk of a place called 'prep school'. They spoke of this place where boys would be able to play cricket and study interesting things like history with lots of other boys of the same age, in a nice seaside town with a bracing English climate. Gradually it dawned upon Paul and me that we were going to be sent to this place and left there. We would not be returning to India with our parents.

As the time for departure drew closer Sholapur became more and more dear to my heart, and my perception of the Indian countryside, the bazaar with its teeming life, and all things Indian, became a vivid and heart-rending experience.

Every evening ride, with the sun setting over the lake[7] and the fireflies beginning to twinkle in the cool of an autumnal dusk, made me aware of what I would be missing. No more would I see the flying foxes as they swooped on the mosquitoes and small insects for their nightly feasts. I would miss the noise and clamour of the stallholders in the bazaar into which we would venture on supervised excursions, with strict instructions never to be tempted to spend our few *annas* of pocket money on the purchase of any of the gooey sweetmeats displayed under a canopy of excited flies.

I wondered what would happen to our ponies, horses and remaining dogs. I could not bear to think that I would never see them again. I would not see Ahmed, or Mina or Lela, Lela whom I loved. What other little boy would have her as his *ayah* now?

The prospect of a sea voyage did nothing to lighten my spirits.[8]

The Horrors of St Leonards

The prep school at St Leonards-on-Sea was, I suppose, no better or worse than many other establishments of those days to which boys were confined, and nearly all contemporaries who were sent to such places remember them with loathing. I loathed my school so much that I have managed to suppress almost all memories of it. I recall little more than a grey, cold

7. It was not actually a lake, but a reservoir created by a dammed stream, and known as the Bund. (RT)

8. George's original typescript does not include any account of the ensuing voyage with the parents to England. (RT)

spell of existence, enlivened only by the holidays Paul and I spent at Woodside with Grandpa and Granny Roche, and especially a wonderful summer holiday in Devon when Granny and Tante rented a holiday house there for the summer.

The Joys of Devon

Our excitement began when we took a cab from Woodside to Paddington station to catch the express to Plymouth, where we took another cab to the ferry terminus and boarded the ferry across the Tamar estuary to Cawsand. This trip resembled a short sea voyage, with spray splashing in our faces. There a wonderful vista of sun-filled days spent running wild opened before us.

We roamed the beaches, shrimping and exploring rock pools for small fish and crabs. Our grandmother had the good sense to let us get on with our exploits without much supervision. Sometimes we met local boys and girls and played games with them. They mocked our accents and sometimes we found it hard to follow their Devon speech.

We went for long walks in the Mount Edgecombe Woods to Rame Head. I remember one occasion when Paul and I had a disagreement about something, which led to fisticuffs. We did not notice a dear old lady approaching who, with a scandalized look said: 'Little boys fighting! Oh I am ashamed of you!' We were so surprised that we stopped fighting to stare at her as she went primly on her way. Then we began laughing and chanting, 'I am ashamed of you,' at one another. Friendly relations were restored and we continued on our way to Rame Head, a point jutting out to sea, which gave us the impression of being on the prow of a ship and brought back nostalgic memories of our voyages to and from India.

We swam almost every day when the tide was in. We often asked a friend of Grandma's whom we met walking along the beach: 'What is the tide doing?' She invariably replied, 'It's on the turn, dearie.' This became another stock joke between Paul and myself. We quoted her words whatever the manifest direction of the tide.

We spent almost all day outside, and had no need for any entertainment in the evenings. We were asleep at dusk and slept till dawn.

All too soon the lovely summer holiday was over and we were back in our bleak prep school with other unfortunate boys whose fathers manned the British Empire beyond the seas.

We wrote regularly to our parents from school. The composition of such letters was compulsory, a special period being set aside for it on Saturday afternoons. On those occasions one or other of the three spinsters who ran the school sat watching over us as we dutifully put pen to paper. We could have complained of our misery to our parents, but it was politic not to do so when Miss Fanny, Miss Lizzie or Miss Polly would read every word we wrote to check our spelling and punctuation.

Since this narrative is intended to concentrate on our experiences of childhood in India, I should not include long passages about life in England when our parents were on long leave, or during our period at the prep school at St Leonards-on-Sea. However, I want to include an account of the Christmas we spent at Woodside. My memory of it is indelibly vivid, and it contrasts greatly with all our memories of India.

The weather was cold and grey, and I was glad to seek the warmth of the kitchen range, where I could watch Grandma and Tante preparing for the forthcoming feast.

It was evident that Christmas puddings were of major importance. Great heaps of dried fruit were mixed into a combination of flour and butter. Pints of stout were poured into the mixture, followed by a good measure of brandy. And, when they considered the time was ripe, various silver coins, numerous threepenny bits, one or two sixpences and even a couple of shillings. Grandma insisted that the coins must be carefully washed before they went into the pudding, just in case there might be any germs on them. If she could have inspected our kitchen in Sholapur she would probably have thrown up her hands in horror.

When the whole mass was considered to be of the right consistency it was turned out into 12 separate pudding basins and tied up with clean cloth coverings, with string. Then they were boiled.

Paul and I enjoyed watching these rituals, especially when whey were conducted in the warmest room in the house, in the depth of winter.

Then the turkey was delivered, a bird which had been carefully scrutinized by Grandma before purchase at a nearby butcher's shop.

Now another ritual took place. Grandma insisted that all sinews must be drawn from the turkey's legs and thighs, which was quite a performance. It involved cutting into the legs, exposing the end of a sinew, winding it on to a skewer and, then, whilst Grandma clutched the turkey to her bosom, Jane, our maid, would heave away at the skewer, pulling it till the sinew was withdrawn. I doubt if such trouble is taken in these days of frozen turkeys. But it made the legs most succulent and tender.

On Christmas morning we woke up to 'sensible' presents, the myth of Father Christmas having long been exploded after we were seven years of age. Pencil boxes and school shoes were now the order of the day, and, if one was very lucky, some money in an envelope in the foot of the stocking one had hung hopefully at the end of the bed.

After all the joy of receiving our presents we ate breakfast and were then rounded up to go to church. The church was within walking distance of the house. After about an hour we wended our way back to enjoy our Christmas lunch. This was attended by several close friends of my grandparents, elderly people whose children had long since grown up and scattered. No children came with these guests. Paul and I were somewhat overawed by the invasion, silently tucking into the memorable meal of turkey, Christmas pudding and mince pies crammed with mincemeat.

The occasion was a decorous one, with the adults chatting soberly and taking their time over it. No one drank much or laughed too loudly, for Christmas had not yet become the Bacchanalian revel of today. Paul and I began to feel restive at sitting still for so long, being seen and not heard. Fortunately Grandpa began to yearn for some exercise at about the same time and offered to take us for a walk. Grandpa walked briskly and we enjoyed the pace, though we were not allowed to run on ahead or skip about. Walking in those days was called 'walking off our animal spirits'.

By the time we returned all the guests were gone. Grandma, Tante and Jane had cleared the table and done the washing up. Paul and I had books to read, or we could play chess. Grandpa had taught us to do this and we enjoyed the game. Christmas day ended on a quiet note at Woodside.

As mentioned briefly at the beginning of this book, Grandpa was a son of Antonin Roche, who had come to England from France in about 1836 or 1837 at the invitation of Lady Stanley of Alderley, who had persuaded him to give lessons to young ladies in London, particularly in French. With her influence, his classes in Cadogan Gardens, Mayfair, were very successful and were attended by many members of the English aristocracy. Grandpa inherited Antonin's classes, but later in the century, by which time girls' schools had become more plentiful. Girls now went to schools instead of to Grandpa's exclusive classes, but, being a gentleman with a small private income, he did not subsequently seek any other employment.

Suddenly, whilst we were at the prep school, we received a letter from our father telling us that we would be leaving the school and going back to India to rejoin our parents at Poona.

I never discovered why our parents made this decision. At the time Paul and I were so overjoyed that it never occurred to us to ponder the matter. Parents of their generation did as they thought fit, whatever others might consider to be in the interests of the children.

We thought our prayers had been answered when we went to Woodside for the Easter holidays and Granny packed our trunks, and hugged and kissed us affectionately. We were going home again.

6

On Our Way: SS *Castalia*

I t was a fine spring day when our grandmother took us to
Tilbury dock and put us aboard the SS *Castalia*, a ship of
the Anchor Line. She took us to meet the chief stewardess, a kindly soul in whose charge we were placed. The chief
stewardess showed us to the cabin allotted to us, and Grandma
came along to inspect it.

Then it was time for Grandma to go ashore. She besaught us
to be good, to obey the stewardess and, above all, to avoid
falling overboard. It was very sad saying goodbye. We knew
she loved us as much as we loved her.

The ship drew away from the dock and Grandma went off in
a cab she had kept waiting for her. We dashed tears from our
eyes and ran off to explore the ship.

The *Castalia*, of some 8000 tons, catered comfortably for
about 80 passengers, whilst transporting some cargo.

The Anchor Line ships were noted for the excellence of
their food. Paul and I did not care what the food was like, nor
what our cabin was going to be like. All we wanted was to get
back to India. These ships thumped along at about ten knots,
and it took about three weeks to get to Bombay from Tilbury,
whereas the P & O ships completed the journey in a fortnight.

My parents always preferred Anchor Line ships to others.
There was a happy, informal atmosphere aboard, no snobbery,

no pecking order of the kind that prevailed when senior army personnel travelled in the same ship as mere captains and their wives.[1]

We explored the ship for kindred spirits, but there were very few children on the *Castalia*. We came upon a little girl whose father was an Anglican vicar in Bombay, and she was going out to join her parents after a stay with her grandparents. We chummed up, but we did not really like girls.

Port Said, Bum Boats and Scimitars

We were hoping for adventures and excitement, but did not get much until we got to Port Said. It was evening when we got there and a hawser was rowed ashore and fastened to a dockside bollard. In the meantime a host of 'bum boats' from the shore were rowing towards the *Castalia*, loaded to the gunwales with what seemed to us fascinating wares, local, hand-made artefacts, toy camels and pouffes of crudely tanned leather with a rather nasty smell, stuffed with goodness knows what.

Passengers leaned over the ship's rails watching these boats, and the hawkers aboard them were already holding up some of their wares and shouting, 'Very cheap!' Whilst this was going on the first mate gave the order to the capstan crew to reel the ship alongside the dock. The hawser was under water and as it tightened it surfaced suddenly and caught the undersides of several of the bum boats unlucky enough to be immediately above it, causing them to flick over, tipping their crews and cargoes into the murky water of the dockside. Camels and pouffes were bobbing about as the hawkers tried desperately to right their boats and salvage their wares. This

---

1. During all the decades of the ocean-going liners, especially those of not more than about 15,000 tons, the majority of passengers were of working age and a large proportion of them were travelling alone. In the course of every voyage new friendships were made and love affairs were virtually *de rigueur*. (RT)

they did remarkably quickly, so I suppose they were accustomed to such mishaps.

As soon as the ship was tied up alongside, swarms of hawkers clambered aboard, grinning hugely over the disaster that had struck their competitors. They began setting out their wares on the deck, but got in the way of the crew who had to discharge some of the cargo. They were moved along, out of the area of the hatches, which had to be opened.

Open hatches attracted Paul and me like magnets, and we too had to be moved along sharply.

We gazed at the treasures of the Orient spread about our feet. Our grandmother had passed on to us our mother's strict instructions not to buy anything from any of the hawkers at any of the ports. However, neither of us wanted a stuffed camel or a pouffe, but I did crave some of the knives on display, particularly a scimitar with a jewel-encrusted handle. Paul fancied it too, admiring the green and red glass 'gems' in the handle. I liked the sharpness of the curved blade. The hawker, unaware of our mother's ban, produced another scimitar exactly the same and held both of them out expectantly. We shook our heads sadly. The hawker probably had dozens of such gaudy weapons in stock.

Soon the stewardess in charge of us came looking for us and ushered us below decks to have supper and go to bed, cautioning us to remain in the safety of the cabin. With open hatches and hawkers about on the deck, who knew what might happen to two small boys? Perhaps the stewardess had not thought of our being kidnapped, but the thought did occur to me, and I was not tempted to disobey her instructions.

After breakfast the next morning we wanted to go ashore, and our stewardess asked a middle-aged couple if they would mind taking us with them. They did not seem very enthusiastic and I suppose the responsibility would have reduced the pleasure of shopping in Simon Artz's huge and famous emporium, where Western travellers confronted fabulous Eastern merchandise — silks, perfumes, golden jewellery, jade and ivory exquisitely carved. Our chaperones wanted to browse over such items undisturbed. Paul and I wanted to watch the fishing boats drawn up at the quayside, laden with the night's catch, a great variety of fish swarming with flies and smelling strongly, however freshly caught. As the *memsahib* would not let us linger we were shunted along to Simon Artz, where almost all the passengers from the *Castalia* had congregated.

The 'Gully-Gully Man'

Back on the ship for lunch we found that the 'gully-gully man' had come aboard and was waiting to perform his conjuring tricks. He must have been disappointed to see so few children, for it was they who most enjoyed his performances. However, after lunch a few passengers gathered in the lounge, some with babies and toddlers. Paul and I and our little girl friend, whom I shall call Mary, having forgotten her real name, were the eldest children.

The gully-gully man went through his repertoire, pulling yards and yards of coloured handkerchiefs out of the original one which he had waved about to show that he was concealing nothing up his sleeves or in any other parts of his clothing. Then he would create many small live yellow chicks out of thin air, and from behind our ears, or the ears of other children. We were not very amused, but I was curious to discover what he did with the chicks whenever he removed them from view. Did they go into a hidden pocket, enabling him to use the same chicks over and over again? Or did he really have dozens of chicks concealed about his person? In any case I felt sorry for the skinny, fluffy little bundles.

The *Castalia* took her place at the back of the queue of vessels waiting to traverse the canal in the late evening, and her search lights illuminated the waters. It was bedtime for us, so we did not see much. The ship was still wending its way through the canal when we woke up. It could be a very slow journey, for the ship might have to anchor in the Bitter Lake to allow another ship going the other way to pass by.

We were through the canal and had entered the Red Sea by the time we had eaten our lunch.

The Red Sea is a hot stretch of salty water about 1500 miles long and 140 miles wide at its widest, but less than 50 miles wide where it flows between Africa and Arabia into the Gulf of Aden. The days we spent in the Red Sea were hot and oppressive. Sometimes a sudden squall can come from the north, but none did so on this occasion, and we sweltered with no breeze to cool us. As we approached the Gulf of Aden and moved through the narrow straits separating Africa and Arabia the whole sea seemed to glow red, and even the African hillsides glowed with a fiery hue.

Bombay at Last

After Aden only a few more days remained before we would reach Bombay. Our excitement at the prospect of seeing our parents and the land of our birth mounted. Boisterously we chased each other up and down the decks, which earned us many a disapproving look from passengers relaxing in long chairs with feet up and books in their laps.

7

Poona

There was the usual milling throng on the quayside at Bombay: so many brown bodies; so few white ones. Where were our mother and father? Not there, not there, but *there*, standing close together, looking up at the ship. We waved frantically in their direction. Would they see us squashed against the rail half hidden by the adult passengers who pressed over us, looking for friends or relatives they hoped would be meeting them?

Yes! My father was waving both his arms over his head and my mother, more gracefully, was waving with one arm. We were impatient to join them and it seemed to take forever before the gangplank was lowered. When it was we charged for it, taking no heed of our stewardess's warning to be careful. 'Goodbye! Goodbye!' and, as an afterthought, 'Thank you for looking after us.'

Then we were down on the quayside, hugging our parents, both talking at once, and for once they did not reprimand us about this. Someone else was also talking, Sylvia. As fast as we said something, so did she. As an early feminist, she was not going to be left out of anything.

We ignored Sylvia and she ignored us. We were anxious to get aboard our father's special railway coach and begin the journey to Poona, where my father had been posted some time before, and where he was very busy designing a grand new station, now nearing completion. At that time it was considered the very last word in stations, with such amenities as restaurants, waiting rooms and offices.

Poona was regarded as one of the prime postings for Great Indian Peninsular Railway officers, and my father was much to be envied.

It was about eight hours' rail journey from Bombay to Poona, and the time passed quickly. We were so full of questions that we hardly noticed the magnificent scenery of the Western Ghats, the forested hills running down the western side of the Indian peninsula, or stopping at a place called Lonavley, beyond which the rail zigzags to mount the steep gradient. We were shaken about as the train jinked over the zigzags.[1]

When we arrived at Poona my father walked across to our house, which stood very close to the station, and fetched the car to take us all home. The car! Our eyes grew round as the Singer Tourer hove into view. How much more desirable than the old 'Indian' motorcycle! And what further wonders awaited us?

My father had been allocated a magnificent semi-circular bungalow in three acres of garden, with a tennis court, stabling and paddocks. Wide verandahs extended round the whole semi-circular structure. The family living quarters took up most of the interior, but at one end of the building a small portion of the arc housed my father's office and those of the *babu*s and *chaprassi*s (clerks and messengers) who dealt with the piles of paperwork.

The Eagle's Nest
The house, called The Eagle's Nest, was situated in Sassoon

1. The zig-zagging mountain railways of India are many, all great feats of civil engineering achieved during the nineteenth century. (RT)

Road. It was approached by a long driveway curving round and upwards to the front entrance. My father stopped the car and we gazed up at the wide stone steps, flanked by ornate stone pillars. These led the way to another elaborate portico on the verandah over the front door of the house.

A Conducted Tour

We were soon scrambling up these steps with Sylvia, who was struggling to get ahead of us and saying: 'I'll show you the way. You don't know this house. I *do*.'

We ignored her and rushed in between the open doors into a huge lounge, through an archway and into the dining room. 'Ahmed! Ahmed! Are you here?' I shouted, and he was. He came in from the kitchen and greeted us with a smile.

'This is my bedroom,' Sylvia was saying, indicating a door that led off the dining room. 'It's all mine and you can't come in unless I say so.'

Then she went to another door, threw it open and said: 'That's your room. You've got to share it. It isn't any bigger than mine.'

But now our mother had arrived on the scene. 'All right, Sylvia, don't get excited,' she said. 'Come on boys and see if you like it.'

The room was almost an exact replica of our bedroom in Sholapur and that was fine with us.

But what about our ponies? Were they all here? Was Rudolf here?

'Rock Honey is my horse,' said Sylvia.

I thought of Rudolf and his spirited performances, and wondered how my parents could have provided my small sister with a horse.

'Rock Honey is a very docile horse,' my mother explained as though reading my thoughts. 'Now you children must get ready for bed. You can go to the stables in the morning.'

Ahmed served us our supper in an alcove off the dining

room and close to the kitchen. Paul and I tucked into our chicken curry, but Sylvia only picked at the small portion he had put on her plate. Seemingly nothing had changed.

But of course many things had changed. Mina and Lela had gone, and the geography of The Eagle's Nest was strange. Tomorrow we would explore every inch of the place.

Horses and Ponies

Early the next morning our first action was to run to the stables. My pony Peggy was there. Rudolf was there. Paul's pony Tansy was there, and a rather spindly chestnut horse was there. Rock Honey.

After breakfast, which we had in the dining room with our parents, my father went to his office and my mother went to sit on the verandah to read magazines, which had arrived on one of the mail ships and had finally reached my father's office in the GIP Railway's private bag.

Paul and I wanted to explore the house, but instead we got a guided tour, Sylvia assuming this responsibility. 'That's Mummy and Daddy's bedroom. It's huge,' she said, pointing to a large room next to the lounge, which fronted onto the verandah. We could see that it was indeed a large bedroom, and we could see our mother sitting outside it reading her magazines with the bedroom doors wide open behind her. She used the bedroom as a sitting room, with an armchair and a small table at which she could write letters or use her sewing machine.

'That's the study.' This room led off the dining room and was between our parents' bedroom and Sylvia's. Our bedroom was next to Sylvia's, and there were three additional bedrooms. 'They are for guests,' Sylvia announced. Next to these bedrooms were two bathrooms, with proper enamelled baths equipped with ball-and-claw feet, and up-to-date hand basins. Cold water was piped to the taps from a large tank outside, and hot water was piped from a tank under which a fire was lit from time to time. All this was luxury indeed. However, the toilets remained the good old 'thunder boxes' of old.[2]

'We can go out this way,' and Sylvia danced through the open door of one of the bathrooms. We followed her into the compound at the back of the house. The servants' quarters were here, always teeming with the families of those who kept our water tanks full (*pani wallahs*), kept our thunder boxes clean (*mehtars*) tended our large garden (*malis*), cleaned our large house (*mehtars*), cooked our food (*khansamans*) and served it. Ahmed, who was both cook and steward, was king here.

The stables were very close so we went to look at the horses again.

'Isn't she lovely?' Sylvia said. And of course she meant the spindly chestnut horse.

Every day, except during the monsoon, we three children went riding before breakfast. Paul and I always outdistanced Sylvia by urging on our horses until we were well ahead of her. She was disadvantaged because she had to be accompanied by a *syce* who was supposed to make sure that she kept her steed to a steady pace. Since the *syce* had to walk, it could

---

2. The traditional 'thunder box' of India was simply a wooden commode, with a seat with a hole in the middle over which people sat to defecate into a pot below. During the Second World War there were, I believe, at least a quarter of a million American troops and auxiliaries in India. They utilized the vast Indian base for valuable operations in support of China against the Japanese who had overrun most of that country. The Americans in their many camps dispensed with 'thunder boxes' as insanitary relics of the British imperial past, and installed thousands of water closets at what we regarded as fabulous expense. One of the consequences was much unemployment among the sweepers (untouchables) of India, whose principal task in life had, since time immemorial, been to empty 'thunder boxes' and keep the pots clean, all of which they accomplished to perfection. (RT)

only amble. We would meet them on the way back, and all go home together for breakfast.[3]

And Turtles

One evening Paul and I were riding our horses towards the club when we came across a group of Indians tormenting two large turtles by prodding them with sticks. The turtles were very ferocious creatures, reacting with fury to the treatment by grabbing the sticks and breaking the ends off them with their powerful jaws.

Paul insisted that we hurry to the club to entreat our parents to rescue the poor turtles. We did so and persuaded them to come and see what was happening. The Indian youths were still tormenting the creatures, which showed no sign of fatigue with snapping off the ends of the sticks. My mother had a very soft spot for all animals and was strongly opposed to cruelty of any kind. She persuaded my father to buy both turtles for a few rupees. In a few seconds they were hoisted upside down upon the backs of their former tormentors and carried along the road to our home, where a temporary pen had to be made for them at very short notice.

3. The annals of the later decades of the Raj include many accounts of horse riding before breakfast, when the air was still cool before the onset of the daily heat. Such rides were facilitated by great stretches of open land with rough tracks over the bare earth, leading between the cultivated areas near villages. Metalled roads for vehicles were built by the civil engineers and military officers of the East India Company gradually from the mid-seventeenth century onwards. Before that pedestrians, bullock carts, elephants, camels, and the great, slow-moving armies of princes moved directly over the land in the dry season. During the monsoon months all such movement was impossible, or greatly restricted, on account of vast areas of flood and, of course, the land was infested with snakes, scorpions and mosquitoes. Despite the vast growth of population, much of the ancient Indian scene still remains, and people still ride before breakfast. India never completely overwhelms her own past. This, I believe, is the quintessential quality of the Indian scene. (RT)

My father called for a couple of our garden labourers who banged in some wooden stakes and draped chicken wire around them, enclosing our new pets inside.

During the next few days a special concrete-lined pond was made for them in the garden, surrounded by a stout wire fence. We fed the turtles on dead rats, which our little fox terrier Lucy used to catch daily, and it was most interesting to see them eating the rats. They would first tear out the rat's stomach and eat it. Then, in a few seconds, the rest of the rat would be completely devoured. Lucy never tired of catching rats, so our turtles were always very well fed.

We had not been aware that our turtles were of opposite sex and as husband and wife they seemed very happy. It was not long before Mrs Turtle laid a number of eggs in the soft sand of the pen, and shortly afterwards numerous small turtles were wandering about in the pen and taking to the water.

When we first made a home for the turtles we had no inkling that we should one day have to return them to the wilds. When that day arrived all the turtles were put in sacks, placed in the Singer and driven to Lake Karakwesla behind a huge dam, which supplied Poona with its water. The sacks were emptied on the lake shore. Father, mother and all the little turtles scuttled off towards the deep lake. We watched them as they swam away until we could see them no more.

Sylvia's Honey

As I said, after our morning rides we returned home for breakfast. Paul and I had graduated to eggs and bacon. Sylvia was allowed to settle for a slice of toast with honey spread on it, which was all she ever wanted.

She liked honey and I remember a day when we went shopping with our mother in the pony trap. Sylvia bought a jar of honey and sat with it on her lap during the journey home.

She was hugging it as she got out of the trap. Paul and I raced up the steep stone steps of the house with Sylvia following. At the top she balanced the jar on her head and chanted 'Mine! All mine!' The jar fell and smashed, honey dripping down the steps. Sylvia resembled the anguished figure of a heroine in a Greek tragedy.

After breakfast came lessons till lunch time, after which our father gave us our French exercise before returning to his office when, at last, we were free. Or not exactly free because our mother insisted that we rested on our beds and kept quiet. Paul found this easier than I did. He enjoyed reading, but I found it wearisome to read whilst lying down, even if the book was full of adventure stories. I wanted to be up and doing something, anything, so long as it was something active. I suppose practitioners of child psychology today would have labelled me as hyperactive, which seems very foolish to people of my generation.

I would go out into the garden and play with a ball, run round the garden, climb a tree. Paul would soon join me and we would knock balls over the tennis net with old rackets discarded by our parents. We called it playing tennis. Sometimes our eyes strayed towards the road, which funeral parties followed. So long as we held rackets in our hands we did not feel that we were disobeying our mother's dictum not to watch any more funerals.

We often had tea in the garden, but more usually on the verandah. Miss Power and Sylvia would join us, but my mother often remained in her bedroom.

At five o'clock we could go to the club. We could walk, or we could ride. Paul and I were allowed to ride alone, but Sylvia had to have Miss Power alongside. Our parents went in the car by themselves.

Life in the Garrison Town

Poona was quite a large town, being both a military headquarters and an important commercial centre. A British regiment always occupied the barracks bordering the *maidan* and officers' bungalows, sheltered by a line of trees, bordered the other side of it.[4]

About two miles from the centre of the town, at Kirkee, was the headquarters of the 17th Lancers (named the Poona Horse), the Bombay Sappers and Miners, and ancillary units. All were smart regiments of Indian troops commanded almost exclusively by British officers.

The shopping centre and bazaar were about a mile from the British regiment's barracks. This centre boasted several good shops, like Whiteways, and two hotels, one of which was called The Cornelia, run by Italians, where we often sat and enjoyed ice creams after our mother had finished her shopping.

The bazaar itself was rather more sophisticated than those usually found in smaller centres, and my mother often went to a Muslim shop called Moosa's, where she could buy lengths of excellent dress material for making up into costumes for day and evening wear.

There was an excellent club at Poona, with facilities for polo, cricket and tennis. It was only half a mile from our house and situated in beautiful surroundings. There was also a Gymkhana Club. Postings to Poona were sought after.

Corpses and Marigolds

We had not been in our house for very long when we found that the side garden of the house near the tennis court over-looked the road used by Hindu funeral processions on their way to the pyres on the banks of the Bhima River for cere-monial burning of the dead. These funeral processions, always preceded by a dirge, held a macabre fascination for Paul and

4. The word *maidan* indicates a large open space of flat land used in the British period, and by former Indian rulers, for ceremonial parades and the routines of training troops of all kinds, and for the similar training of police and bandsmen. It was also often used as a shooting range for small arms training. (RT)

me. Standing on the tennis court we could see the pall bearers carrying the stretchers on which lay the corpses, uncovered but for garlands of marigolds.

Sometimes, when some epidemic had taken a severe toll of the Indian population, these processions seemed interminable. Paul and I began to have a phobia about death and germs, imagining that the air around the corpses would be full of the most dreadful germs ready to make a beeline for us standing only 50 yards away, gazing at the scene in mute horror. It did not stop us from watching, however.

We were incautious enough to describe these grisly scenes to Sylvia, and she told our mother. We were forbidden to watch any more funerals.

Miss Power and Lessons
It was not long after this that my father arranged to keep us occupied for most of the day. Miss Power, a pleasant, plain Eurasian woman was engaged to give us lessons. Actually, she gave Sylvia lessons, but supervised Paul and me as we read books prescribed by our father and wrote out endless passages to improve our skills in writing. We also solved the sums and problems set out in an arithmetic book he had bought especially for us. The book had answers at the back, which made supervision essential to prevent cheating. History and geography books, together with Stevenson's *Treasure Island*, *Kim* and other tales by Kipling, were also acquired. However, even such fiction was considered frivolous, and less time was spent over it than on history and geography. 'If you want to read for pleasure, you can do it in your spare time,' pronounced our father.

From 10 a.m. to 12.30 p.m. we sat in the study with Miss Power. Sylvia was allowed to escape from her endeavours to unravel such monosyllabic mysteries as 'the cat sat on the mat', and the very low multiplication tables, which were learnt by heart in those days.

We children, Miss Power and our parents took lunch together in the dining room, after which our father instructed us in French grammar — our verbal French was already very good — and then assigned to us a French novel to read. He would question us about it, often during lunch, on some later occasion.

Miss Power lived with the family and was given the bedroom next to mine and Paul's. Her father was a ticket inspector on the railway, and her home was in the 'railway lines' not far away. On most afternoons she went home, to the shops or the bazaar, but whatever she did she was always back by 4.30 p.m. to accompany us children to the club, to which our parents almost always went at 5.00 p.m.

Bhima River, Temples and Pyres

On Saturdays there were no lessons, and sometimes after breakfast we would ride our respective steeds to the bank of the Bhima River, along which were numerous small but very ornate Hindu temples. We would like to have looked inside them, but our parents said that they were holy places and that it would be disrespectful for us to tramp into them merely to look round.[5]

5. In India all rivers, lakes and the sea itself are regarded as holy. The immersion of the body and washing are acts of ritual no less than of personal hygiene. The availability of water, however, varies not only with the seasons but in different parts of the sub-continent. In the driest regions, where there is very little water apart from that pulled laboriously from deep wells, many of the gestures of washing are purely symbolic. But in heavy rainfall areas, such as much of Bengal, the south-east and south, the people keep themselves wonderfully clean by frequent ritualistic immersions. Many Indian and Pakistani Muslims share with the Hindus a reverence for water. The importance of baptism in the Christian world is no doubt associated with the aridity of much of the Middle East, in which the religion had its origins. (RT)

However, elsewhere we saw many men and women chastely clad immersing themselves in the river, running their hands over themselves to rinse off dust and grime. We also saw women and *dhobi*s washing garments upon suitable rocks to cleanse them. It was very rough on the garments. But are not some washing machines as rough on garments?

When on the river bank we could usually see in the distance smoke rising from funeral pyres. We were still fascinated by them, but never ventured too close because we had been told that when the flames reached the skull it burst with a loud bang.

Catholic Cathedral and British Cemetery

On Sundays we went to the Roman Catholic cathedral. To get there we had to drive past the *maidan* and the British regiment's barracks. From the windows of the Singer we could see the soldiers sprucing themselves up for church parade. I felt sorry for these men who were as far removed from home as I had been at my hated prep school, but perhaps they had chosen their way of life and did not mind it.

A regimental band was usually playing, and the boundaries of the *maidan* were always thronged with onlookers waiting for the parade to begin.

At the Catholic cathedral we heard Mass in company with other Catholics, Europeans, Eurasians and Indians, and the cathedral was always full.

Further away was the British cemetery, where the dead of other denominations were interred. Some of the graves went back more than a century. I have always been interested in cemeteries, especially those in faraway places. Even in those days I wanted to look at old tombs and read the inscriptions, but we were always whisked off home very quickly.

Guests would often join us for Sunday lunch. If they included important people, such as the general manager of the railway on a visit from Bombay, we would not have to join them at table. Ahmed would serve us in our alcove. We could eat quickly and scamper off to our bedrooms, into the garden, or into the servants' compound.

More Mischief

After such 'business lunches' our parents were exhausted and went straight to their bedrooms to rest in the hottest spell of daylight. And at such times Paul and I felt free to examine the car closely. We knew better than to try to start it; we did not want a repetition of the 'Indian' incident, but we wanted to find out how to make the hood go up and down. It was very simple really. All we had to do was to unscrew a couple of wing nuts on the windscreen and the canvas hood would collapse backwards. We achieved this objective, but before we could return the hood to its correct position our father appeared on the scene, and asked angrily why we could not leave things that did not belong to us alone. We mumbled: 'Sorry, we only wanted to sit in the car and try to make the roof open and shut.' He stomped off saying severely: 'Well don't ever do it again.'

We were never very interested in any of our parents' guests and they were not at all interested in us, which suited us very well.

Cricket and the Great Man

But we did look forward with great excitement to the arrival of one particular guest. Soon after we arrived in Poona the MCC sent out a team to play cricket against various Indian teams, and D. R. Jardine, the captain of the MCC team, was going to stay with us because my mother had known him in England when she was a girl.

The great man ate breakfast with us, unperturbed by my unwavering stare of admiration, and since we children were not allowed to speak at the table unless we were spoken to, I could not tell him how much I enjoyed cricket.

The matches were played at the Poona Club cricket ground, and almost the entire local population, Indian, Eurasian and European, lined the boundaries to watch them.

Some spectators had taken folding chairs to sit upon, but most people sat on the grass or stood. My parents were sitting on chairs and my mother had her parasol with her to shade her head. Paul and I were sitting in front of her, standing up every now and again to get the circulation going again in our legs. Every time we did so we were told to 'sit down and keep still'.

I greatly enjoyed the matches. I remember one MCC batsman who thumped sixes and fours all round the field, much to my mother's alarm, for she thought her parasol would not provide much protection against a high-velocity cricket ball if one came her way.

There were dances and parties at the club after the matches to entertain the visitors, but we were at home with Miss Power long before they began, and sound asleep before my parents and our distinguished guest returned to the bungalow.

I do not think I said much more than 'Hello' and 'Goodbye' to the man I so much admired.

Branch Line to Akalkot

A year or two before Paul and I had got to Poona, my father had become a close friend of the rajah of the small Maratha princely state of Akalkot, about a day's journey by road to the south-east of Poona.

The friendship probably developed during negotiations about the practicability of constructing a branch line to Akalkot from some point on the main line of the Great Indian Peninsular Railway, partly or wholly at the expense of the princely state. The rajah, who had been educated at Oxford and had spent much of his time abroad, believed that the rail extension would bring benefits to the state. Nothing came of the proposal, however.

Four Days at the Palace

One day my father told us that the rajah had invited us all to stay at his palace at Akalkot for a long weekend which, coinciding with a national holiday, meant that we should be there for almost four days. We were very excited and apprehensive at having to be on our very best behaviour for so long.

The palace was about 50 miles away and we went there in the Singer. It seemed a long way, for the road was only a bullock cart track and caution was needed to avoid ruts and pot holes. Even on good roads the maximum speed of the Singer did not exceed about 35 miles per hour which, in any case, my mother considered excessive.

As we approached the state boundary we could see that the plain surrounding the palace was teeming with herds of black buck and other game. These animals were protected, in the sense that only the rajah himself might shoot them, and since he did so only rarely, they were able to multiply plentifully.

Looming out of the heat haze ahead of us we saw what appeared to be a magical oasis full of large shady trees and a lake dotted with small islands, the whole scene dominated by magnificent buildings.

The whole estate was bounded by a high wall, and we entered through a large archway. A major-domo in a splendid uniform greeted us most courteously, directing my father to stop the car in the palace courtyard. When we had alighted a chauffeur appeared as if from nowhere and drove the Singer away to park it out of sight at the back of the guest wing in which we were to stay. The rajah had two yellow Rolls-Royces and I wondered what his chauffeur thought about having to drive our humble vehicle.

The major-domo led us up some marble steps into a very large square entrance hall with colourful tiles on the floor and ornately decorated walls. Then he disappeared through a doorway, to reappear a few minutes later followed by the rajah.

He was a tall, athletic-looking man, a Maratha with a handsome face dominated by a sweeping moustache. He shook my father by the hand, greeting him warmly. My father introduced my mother and the three children.

As soon as the greetings were over the major-domo conducted us through a long corridor to the suite of rooms reserved for us in the guest wing. They were splendidly adorned, with Persian and Indian rugs spread over the tiled floors and elegant electric light fittings of brass glittering on the walls. The palace had its own power generator.

Cucumber Sandwiches

When we had washed the dust from our bodies in the luxurious bathroom we went into the sitting room and found the major-domo presiding over a silver teapot and a huge plate of wafer-thin cucumber sandwiches, the fare that the English were assumed to relish in every corner of the world in mid-afternoon. Paul and I were entranced.

The major-domo poured the tea into bone china cups and my mother watched anxiously as we balanced these delicate vessels in one hand whilst holding sandwiches in the other. We ate fast, dropping crumbs on the lovely rugs.

Rajah and Rani, Vijay and Nina

After we had disposed of the tea and every single sandwich, the rajah came to ask if we were comfortable and had everything we wanted. (What more could we possibly have wanted?) He then suggested we might like to stroll in the palace grounds, and then take a walk round the lake in which there were some huge carp. We were all keen to do this.

At the lakeside we found the rani and her two children already there. The boy, Vijay, was about a year older than me and his sister, Nina, about the same age as Paul. We eyed each other with the wariness of all children who meet for the first time, and none of us said very much.

Carp, Peacocks, Ceilings of Gold

We relaxed, however, when the rajah showed us how the carp came up to the surface to take titbits of boiled rice from his hand. Soon all the children were dipping their fingers into the earthenware pot containing the rice and offering grains to the carp, which swam up to take them.

Around the lake strutted numerous peacocks. Every now and then they uttered their strangely mournful cries. We envied Vijay and Nina their dominance over such a place as this.

All too soon it was time to go indoors and for us children to eat supper and get ready for bed. Our parents were to dine privately with the rajah and rani in the palace.

When our parents left the suite we amused ourselves by switching the lights off and on. When they were on the gilded ceiling with its cherubs carved upon it glowed. We enjoyed plunging this panoramic display into darkness and then suffusing it with light.

Paul and I had brought books with us and I took mine to bed with me to enjoy the novelty of reading by electric light in bed at night.

From the inside of the mosquito net the gilded ceiling veiled by the gauzy net looked as I imagined heaven would appear as one is being wafted up into it. It was much more pleasant to gaze upon than the cloth ceiling in the house we had lived in at Sholapur. I read for a while and then, since Paul had fallen asleep, I got out of bed and switched off the light, and fell asleep quickly myself.

When I awoke the ceiling was aglow in the morning sunlight, another breathtaking spectacle.

After breakfast my father went off with the rajah to shoot buck, and my mother took us out in the palace grounds where the rani was waiting with Vijay and Nina who, their mother said, had something special to show us. She then walked off with my mother.

111

And the Cheetah

Vijay and Nina looked solemnly at us, and we looked solemnly at them.

'What is it, then?' said Sylvia impatiently.

'A cheetah,' said Vijay proudly. We were impressed.

'Come on and show us then,' urged Sylvia.

They led us through the grounds to an enclosure at some distance from the palace. Inside were cages containing jackals and others with monkeys. A little apart from them was a magnificent cage and inside it sat a very splendid cheetah. It wore a very fine wide collar studded with semi-precious stones. It yawned at us, stood up and began to prowl round the cage.

'What a beautiful animal,' I said.

'Yes,' agreed Vijay, 'but you should see him run. He is the fastest animal alive.'

'He can't run in that cage,' said Sylvia, 'and if you let him out he'd run away.'

'We do let him out, and he doesn't run away,' said Vijay scornfully.

'Why not?' asked Sylvia.

'I will tell you,' said Vijay, and this is what he told us.

The rajah liked to exercise the cheetah by taking it out to hunt black buck. Whenever such a hunt took place the cheetah's handler entered its cage and slipped a stout lead on to its collar. He then led the cheetah to a bullock cart, put him inside and got in with him. The cart was covered with a canvas cover supported by a framework of hoops, and the back of the cart was open. The handler blindfolded the cheetah, put a hand on its back and made it sit, stroking it soothingly, keeping it calm and quiet.

Then the bullocks pulled the cart along towards the open plain where the black buck were grazing. The buck were so accustomed to bullock carts that they were never alarmed at their approach.

When the cart containing the cheetah was about 100 yards from the buck, the handler would remove the blindfold from the cheetah's eyes and slip its leash. With one bound the cheetah was out of the cart and streaking after the herd. The buck sped off, but the cheetah always caught up with one of the unfortunate animals. With a final spring it would bring it to the ground and grab its throat, killing it almost instantly.

The rest of the herd would disappear in all directions. The handler would run up to the cheetah, slip its leash on again and drag it away from its prey. Someone else would load the carcass on to another cart, and the cheetah would be driven back to its cage.

If the buck had a particularly fine pair of horns they would be mounted and put in the trophy room of the palace. The meat would make venison, or be fed to the cheetah at its usual feeding time.

We were suitably impressed by this story, and gazed upon the cheetah with respect for its powers as well as its beauty.

I was loth to leave the cheetah, but Paul wanted to see the monkeys, and Sylvia to see the otters, which lived in a specially constructed concrete pool.

Vijay, having told us his story, relapsed into silence, and Nina did not chatter. Their dignified and quiet behaviour served to subdue our natural exuberance, and we followed them demurely back to the guest suite, where they left us outside it.

Vijay and Nina had a governess, Miss Moxon, about 40 years of age, who was a graduate of Oxford University. I suspected that Vijay and Nina were much better educated than the three young Roches.

After we had paid more visits to the palace we became less awed by Vijay and Nina, and they less shy of us. But on that first visit we spent our time together rather tamely walking in the grounds, feeding the carp, going back frequently to the little zoo — Paul to watch the monkeys, I to see the cheetah.

Back at home in Poona we vied with each other in telling Miss Power all about the rajah's palace, and chattered about peacocks and gilded ceilings, with never a thought that Miss Power might envy a lifestyle she was not likely to experience. Or wish that she was white like ourselves, or Indian like the rajah. We had not yet come to realize that in India not everyone was as happy as we were.

The Horse Show
Happy we were indeed as we prepared for the Poona Horse Show. My mother had entered me on Peggy and Sylvia on Rock Honey. Paul had no wish to be entered for the show.

Sylvia and I practised over and over again, trotting, cantering, walking and executing figures of eight around markers set in the ground.

When the great day came our horses were groomed to perfection by our *syce*. Peggy's mane was beautifully plaited, and Rock Honey's coat gleamed. As she had grown she had filled out, and really looked very good.

Our parents with Paul drove to the Gymkhana Club in the Singer, and Sylvia and I, decked out in riding jackets and jodhpurs, wearing topis on our heads, rode our mounts to the club.

Prizes for George and Sylvia
The children's events were held first, and I was soon summoned to give my performance, which must have gone down very well. For, after all the other children in my class had completed their performances, I was adjudged to have come first, and Sylvia came first in her class. I was awarded a large red rosette.

Rock Honey performed perfectly for Sylvia and our parents were very proud of both of us.

Some of the adult events were very exciting, as when cavalry regiments demonstrated their skills in tent-pegging:

thundering along at great speed with lances lowered, they pierced wooden pegs planted in the ground, ripping them up and displaying them impaled on their points to the admiring crowd. I found these displays most thrilling.

When all the events had been won, and when everyone had eaten picnic lunches or, like ourselves, had eaten in style in the club along with the governor of the presidency of Bombay, who was honouring us with his presence, the trophies were presented.

The governor presented them and I received a silver cup from his hands. It stands on my mantelpiece today, a receptacle for a few carnations or roses. The words engraved upon it are:

POONA HORSE SHOW, 1926
1ST PRIZE PEGGY, RIDDEN
BY GEORGE ROCHE

It needs dusting.

Sylvia also received her first prize from the governor. A silver mug, I think it was.

Christmas to Come

After the excitement of the horse show we had Christmas to look forward to. The round of parties began early in December, for the adults, that is. Night after night my parents went out, my mother looking beautiful as always in her evening dresses and smelling of tantalizing perfume.

Sometimes my parents gave the parties, and the Christmas routine was very much as it was at Sholapur. The Christmas tree in the club sparkled with decorations and the party for children was organized by young wives and subalterns.

But I was getting too old to pretend that I still believed in Father Christmas. Sylvia enjoyed it all immensely, for she was pretty and old ladies thought her 'a dear little thing'. She collected a lot of personal gifts from such admirers. Paul and I were not so engaging and somewhat averse to elderly ladies anyway, especially when they leaned over us, breathing huskily.

The Children's Party with Donkeys

At Christmas 1926 our parents gave a children's party in our garden. Paul and I wanted it to be a lively affair, and so they had arranged to hire half a dozen donkeys from a local charcoal burner who used them for carrying sacks of charcoal. After a good rub down by our *syces* the donkeys were ready to transport children wearing party clothes. The highlight of the party was supposed to be the donkey race. Most of the children were delighted with the idea and jumped eagerly on to the donkeys' backs. Unfortunately they were used to transporting charcoal at a very sedate pace and could not be coaxed readily into streaking across the lawn. However, by dint of slapping them on their backsides and shouting 'giddy-up', we did get them to move at more than a walking pace, so every heat produced a winner. Prizes were distributed and the winners were happy enough with them.

However, these events were somewhat spoiled by an accident. One donkey suddenly got the idea that he was supposed to run just when a timid little boy had been placed on his back. The donkey shot forward unexpectedly and the child fell off and broke his arm. His mother became hysterical before taking him off to see a doctor. The accident was soon forgotten, but my mother felt responsible for it and for all the other children gathered at her house.[6]

---

6. The Christmas season, when the climate in most of India is at its best, was an occasion for garden parties of many kinds, and still is. (RT)

To Mahabeleshwar

My father now began to talk about taking some local leave with the whole family at Mahabeleshwar.

We set off for that place in the Singer, full of excitement for two reasons. We had heard that it was a really lovely hill station on the crest of the Western Ghats and, even more important, we were going to stay in a hotel.[7] My mother was delighted not to have to take provisions, bedding, dogs or servants with us. It was 1927 and fashions were changing fast. My mother looked nice in short skirts and both parents were keeping pace with all the latest 'twenties' ideas, far from London. We felt carefree.

We crossed the rather bleak plains around Poona and then started to climb the escarpment leading to the plateau at the top of the Ghats. As we did so the whole nature of the vegetation changed. Arid scrub was replaced by a greener scene. At about tea time we reached the 5000-foot level, and drove along beneath large deodars and pine trees to the hotel.

7. Hotels, as known in Europe and the Western world, existed only in the great cities of India and the larger hill stations, and there are still few of them today. Catering for short-stay travellers and miscellaneous officials (usually Europeans) who did not put up with friends living in the neighbourhood was normally provided by personal servants. These, bringing food, cooking equipment and blankets with them, travelled with their employers in various vehicles in a regular convoy. Travellers stayed in special buildings called *dak* bungalows or circuit houses, sparsely furnished by the Public Works Departments of the various provinces or other authorities. Similar systems prevailed in the overseas dependencies of the other imperial powers. When I travelled in Bihar and Orissa in 1980, I made use of similar official accommodation, but catering was much more difficult than it had been in the years of the British Raj. Indian officials travelling on duty usually stayed with friends or, if they made use of such facilities for sleeping, usually dined with their local friends. (RT)

A Real Hotel

The hotel was like an English country house, with a very friendly atmosphere. Tea was served in a lounge with chintz-covered armchairs and small tables. We children ravenously devoured hot scones spread with raspberry jam made with fruit that grew in the hotel garden.

After tea we went for a walk in the woods around the hotel, marvelling at the height of the trees, which seemed so much taller than those we had seen elsewhere in India.

There were only a few other guests and we were allowed to eat dinner with our parents, a rare treat, after which we were packed off to bed. Our parents took coffee in the lounge and when someone put a record on the gramophone, began dancing. We did not hear them come to bed.

Next day after breakfast we went for another walk, quite a long one, taking a picnic lunch provided by the hotel. We made for a viewpoint from which, so the hotel manager had said, the sea was visible on clear days. When we reached it we were not able to see the distant coastline because of the heat haze. This, however, whetted my father's appetite for the sight of it.

Down to the Sea and the Blazing Sun

My mother did not share his enthusiasm when, the next day, he proposed that we should all drive down to the sea itself. We children gave him all the support he needed to ensure that she came with us.

On the outward journey we freewheeled downhill most of the way till we reached the coastal plain.

By now it was midday and a fierce sun was overhead, causing the heat to strike back at us from rocks bordering the road. In those days everybody wore topis when venturing into hot sunlight for any length of time. Even so, we felt uncomfortable, for the atmosphere became both humid and very hot near the sea.

At last we reached the arid, bare coastline, devoid of trees or even bushes to break the glare reflected from the sea. We ate our picnic lunch in the car beneath the limited shelter of the canvas hood, leaving the doors and windows open, but still sweltered.

As soon as we had eaten and drunk tea from a thermos flask we drove to a scrubby village to search for petrol, for my father said we should need a full tank to negotiate the steep gradient all the way back to Mahabeleshwar in bottom gear.

We found a hand-operated pump and my father requested that our tank be filled up.

All went well till we reached the first uphill stretch. Then the engine started coughing and the car went along in a series of jerks.

My mother complained, with good reason, that the heat was overpowering, and was getting still worse.

My father diagnosed dirt in the carburettor and said he would deal with it. In those days the engines of cars were fairly basic and carburettors comparatively simple. He got out his tools and cleaned it. 'That should do it,' he said. Alas not so. The car started and stopped, started and stopped, in another series of jerks.

'That petrol we got in the village must have been filthy,' he said. 'Something in it must be causing the blockage some-where, because petrol is obviously not getting through to the engine.'

It meant that we had to check the whole pipeline connecting the petrol tank with the engine, taking out sections of the pipe and blowing through each of them. I helped my father with this, but it was a lengthy process.

Mother became increasingly anxious. 'We'll never get back tonight,' she moaned and Sylvia, sensing her mood, whimpered.

My father and I continued blowing hard down each section of the pipe till at last, from one of them, out popped a ball of

119

cotton waste that had acted as a plug, preventing fuel from reaching the engine.

We painstakingly reconnected all the pipes and when we had climbed back into the car my father started the engine, which came smoothly to life.

By now it was late afternoon and we still had about two hours of steady uphill climbing ahead of us.[8] We reached the hotel as dusk was falling. We all had baths and felt much better after a very good dinner.

Next morning my mother was adamant that we were not going on any more long explorations by car, and certainly not descending from the plateau.

An Ice-Cold Swim
Our hosts told us that there was a wonderful walk to a waterfall about two miles away. It was indeed a lovely walk through a cool forest, and it was not long before we could hear water cascading from a cleft between rocks. We came upon an enchanting scene: a clear crystal stream of water falling into a pool surrounded by maidenhair ferns.

Mother dipped her toes into the pool and paddled at the edge of it, but we followed father's example, stripping off all our clothes and swimming in the icy water until she called us to come out before we froze to death.

We obeyed, for we were all numb. Having no towels, we could only run about on the banks to get ourselves dry. Mother had brought a travelling rug for us to sit on during the picnic. All of us made a dive for it, father winning easily. 'Dry Sylvia,' mother ordered.

After Sylvia, Paul had to be dried. Some years before, at Mussoorie, Paul had caught pneumonia after swimming in a similar icy pool, and had nearly died in a hospital there. We

8. In India and all countries lying between the tropical zones darkness falls throughout the year between about 6.00 and 7.00 p.m. (RT)

remembered the anxiety of that time, when the family had waited till 'the crisis' had passed. (See Chapter 5, p.61.) Father and I were dried by the sun. We all ran about chasing each other till we were nice and warm.

We all lay down in the ferns whilst mother opened the picnic basket and distributed its contents. We enjoyed this idyllic spot so much that we returned to it the next day.

On some days we did not leave the hotel grounds, which contained a couple of tennis courts on which our parents played.

I remember those days as a very happy spell, apart from the trip to the coast and the blocked petrol tube. We had no desire to return to Poona.

To Ellora, Siva, Sakti and Nandi and Rudra

My father still had some local leave left and very much wanted to see the Ellora caves, famous for the huge sculptures carved out of the stone walls of the caves themselves.

The sculptures are very erotic but hold a meaningful place in the immense complexity of Indian mythology. Such figures as that of Siva, with his Sakti, a half-man and half-woman composite, riding on the bull Nandi, with its seductive, single-breasted torso, are depicted.

Another sculpture is that of Rudra, the Vedic god of storms, a combination of terrible and beneficent qualities. Many of his attributes were later bestowed upon Siva, particularly in his role as the Destroyer.

In childhood, of course, I knew nothing about all this. My father did, however, know quite a bit about it. Presumably he thought it would be edifying for us to become aware of important features of Indian culture and history.

To visit the caves we travelled in an ordinary railway coach on a local line, and it took us about two hours to reach the station of Ellora. Then we had to walk up a dusty incline for about half a mile to reach them.

121

It was awesome, even terrifying, to be dwarfed by so many huge carvings. I shivered in the cool, gloomy atmosphere, and was glad when our parents had had enough of it. Outside in the sunshine we children ran down the incline towards the station with a sense of relief.

Under a tree not far from the station we sat on the ground and ate our picnic lunch, moving to the station platform only when we could see the train approaching.

Back at home by late afternoon, we bombarded Miss Power with descriptions of the carvings, and she listened good humouredly, as always.

My mother complained of a headache and went to lie down. The headache did not go away and she became ill, very ill, with smallpox.

I can write only a few words about that harrowing time. We prayed endlessly, but our prayers were not answered. Our beautiful mother died ravaged by the terrible disease.

There were fears that all of us might fall ill, but they meant little to us. We were exhausted by weeping and grief. Our father suffered acutely, having lost the wife he loved. When it became clear that none of us could be incubating the disease, he got compassionate leave from the Great Indian Peninsular Railway and took us back to England.

My mother lies in the cemetery near the Catholic cathedral in Poona.

1940. Troop Train Passed Through

I did not return to India until 1940, when I was in the army. Our troop train passed through Poona station, but did not stop.

Note on George Roche's Ancestry

This information is derived from elaborate genealogical tables assembled by George Roche's cousin Henry Roche. These give abundant details of names, dates and other facts of interest. The tables include many talented individuals and titled persons, some of whom are still household names.

George's great-grandfather on his father's side was Antonin Roche de la Beaume, who was born at Solignac-sur-Loire, near Le Puy, in 1810. He was the son of Dominic de la Beaume, whose ancestry can be traced back as far as 1484, and Thérèse Bertrand, whose ancestry can be traced back to 1683.

In about 1837 Antonin Roche moved to London, where he met and, on 10 September 1846, married Emily Mary Moscheles. She was the daughter of the pianist and composer Isak (Ignaz) Moscheles, born in Prague in 1794, and Charlotte Embden, a member of a well-known Hamburg family. Among Charlotte's relations were the poet Heinrich Heine and the Lehmann family (the descendants of a branch of the Lehmann family which moved to England in the nineteenth century include the novelist Rosamond Lehmann, the actress Beatrix Lehmann and the political writer John Lehmann). Charlotte and Isak Moscheles moved to London about 1825.

Before his arrival in London, Antonin Roche had run a highly successful college in Paris, teaching young aristocratic English people (mostly girls — there were few girls' schools in Britain at the time) to speak, read and write cultivated French, an accomplishment especially valued throughout the last century. His achievements were recognized by his appointment as a Chevalier of the Légion d'Honneur. An English lady persuaded him to move the college to London, where it was equally successful, continuing to number the children of the wealthy and the aristocratic among its pupils. Antonin later became a British subject.

Emily Roche died on 21 January 1889 and Antonin ten years later, on 9 July 1899. Their great-grandson George was born at Manmad, near Nasik, in India in 1915.

(R.T.)

Editorial Epilogue

The numerous princely states of India were abolished in 1949–50 by the newly independent government in New Delhi. Readers may wish to know what became of the rajah of Akalkot and his family. The facts are difficult both to ascertain and to record in a book available to the public, such as this. First, there appear to be no official records of such matters. And second, many of the records preserved by the India Office Library and Records are of a confidential nature, including those about Akalkot in particular. Such records take the story down to mid-1947, shortly before India became independent. Information about the subsequent lives of princely rulers, especially those of small states like Akalkot, must be derived almost wholly from private sources. George Roche, living in retirement at the village of Underberg in Natal, was not in a position to unravel the facts. In London I was in a better position for the purpose.

The Roche family's visits to the guest wing of the palace at Akalkot took place between about the year 1920 and 1922. In 1923 the rajah who had been their host died and was succeeded by his wife, the dowager rani, who administered the state as regent on behalf of her son Vijay who, it will be remembered, was the same age as George, both boys having been born in 1915. In 1936 Vijay became 21 years of age and succeeded as rajah with full powers, except that he was required by the British political officer (resident at Kolapur) to consult his mother about important matters of policy.

In his memoir George describes only two royal children at the palace, Vijay and his sister Nina. Nina's real name was Leela, and Vijay had another sister Pramilla, and a younger brother whose name was Jaysingh. The dowager rani died in 1943.

Both sisters married the princes of similar states in the Deccan area. Leela became the rani of the state of Jath and Pramilla married the prince of Kagal. Jaysingh now lives in a suburb of Poona called Model Colony. Vijay died in 1952 when he was only 37 years old, but I have been unable to discover either the cause or the exact date of his death.

Readers may wish to know what became of the palace of Akalkot itself. There were in fact two palaces, old and new respectively. The old one still contains the princely armoury and former residences of the family. The new palace now houses three colleges — the C. D. Kedgi College of Science, the Raje Vijaysingh College of Commerce and the Raje Jaysingh College of Arts. The new palace included a bungalow for the British governess Miss Moxon and residences for members of the staff.

The family name of the princes of Akalkot is Bhosle, and the full name of Vijay was Vijaysingh Fatesingh Raje Bhosle.

The reader is invited to refer to the Acknowledgements to discover the sources of the above information.

The last sentence of George's memoir is: 'Our troop train passed through Poona station and did not stop.' That was in 1940.

The sentence is deeply emotive. His father Robert had personally designed the station itself and was most proud of his achievement. I recall it myself for, early in 1943, whilst in a vast transit camp, under canvas, at Deolali, a few miles away, I was sent in a truck to the British Military Hospital at

Poona for treatment of a minor form of dysentery. In a few days of antibiotic injections I recovered and was allowed to explore Poona. I visited the excellent railway station, the Gymkhana Club, the bazaar and all the shops mentioned by George. All, at that critical stage in the war, were strangely silent and deserted. Poona seemed a ghost town. Men were elsewhere, on the Eastern front, in the Western desert and the Middle East, or in camps closer to the theatres of war.

In the troop train George would have thought, above all, of his mother and former home, and recalled her grave. Was there a commemorative stone at the site and, if so, what inscription would it bear? I decided to search for her grave, but to say nothing to George about my search unless it were successful.

Roberta Roche was buried in the Faith Sulpice cemetery on the Sholapur Road in Poona. Her grave is surmounted by a simple white marble cross. The inscription, perfectly legible after 64 years, is as follows:

RIP

in

LOVING MEMORY

of my darling wife

And our sweet

MUMMY

ROBERTA MARY MICHAEL ROCHE

whom Jesus took on

February 16th 1927

Born September 1890

———

Thou ornamentedst her

Making her reverently amiable

Glossary

ayah	Woman employed to look after small children, in both Indian and European households.
bearer	Head servant, corresponding roughly to a butler. Sometimes known as a steward. Apart from supervising other servants, he waited at table. In European houses he was usually a Muslim who, unlike most Hindus, did not object to meat.
cantonment	Area near a town set aside for soldiers, both Indian and European.
compound	Area, usually behind an officer's house, containing the servants' kitchen and living quarters.
dhobi	Washerman.
Indian	Trade name of a motorcycle widely used in the Indian Army. (As a divisional liaison officer I travelled long distances upon one of them in India during the Second World War. (RT)
maidan	Large open space in or near a town, used for parades and other functions (see footnote 4, p. 79).
MCC	Middlesex County Cricket Club. Despite its name it is widely regarded as the most representative cricket team in England.

syce	Groom.
tonga	Light trap pulled by a pony or horse, entered by steps at the back and able to carry about four adults, apart from the driver, who sat in front with his legs outside the vehicle.
wallah	Common expression meaning 'fellow' or 'fella' associated with a vocation. For example, *pani-wallah*, or water carrier (see footnote 6, p. 79).
Western Ghats	Line of mountains bordering the western side of the Deccan. Many parts are covered with mixed jungle, including thorny bamboo, many rivers and waterfalls. It was a great relief to find that the bamboo of the Arakan was *not* thorny.

Index

131

132

Index